D1567753

Crossing the Circle at
the Holy Wells of Ireland

Crossing the Circle at

University Press of Virginia

Charlottesville and London

the Holy Wells of Ireland

Walter L. Brenneman, Jr.

Mary G. Brenneman

THE UNIVERSITY PRESS OF VIRGINIA
Copyright © 1995 by the Rector and Visitors
of the University of Virginia

First published 1995

Library of Congress Cataloging-in-Publication Data
Brenneman, Walter L.
    Crossing the circle at the holy wells of Ireland / Walter L.
Brenneman, Jr., Mary G. Brenneman.
        p.   cm.
    Includes index.
    ISBN 0-8139-1548-1
    1. Holy wells—Ireland. 2. Folklore—Ireland. 3. Mythology,
Celtic. 4. Ireland—Religious life and customs. 5. Ireland—
Antiquities. I. Brenneman, Mary G. II. Title.
GR153.5.B74   1995
291.3′5′09415—dc20   94-18909
                                                             CIP

Printed in the United States of America

To the people of Ireland who showed us places, gave time, and opened their hearts to this project.

Contents

Illustrations

Acknowledgments

For grants awarded over the years, grateful thanks to the Center for Research, Earthwatch, and the University of Vermont.

Thanks to readers of the early pages: Stan and Lucy Yarian, Dáithí Ó hÓgáin, and Bill Paden. Heartfelt thanks also to Hope Greenberg and Sharon Bernard who did battle with our computer monster, Bill Dilillo of the U.V.M. photo lab, Shams Mortier, mapmaker, and our photographer, Michael Gray.

Special thanks also to the many Earthwatch volunteers, unfortunately too numerous to name, whose research assistance saved us many years in the field. You know who you are!

Lastly, to our acquisitions editor, Cathie Brettschneider, our heartfelt thanks. Only she knows what we shared on this path.

"The difference between the Americans and the Irish is that we still have time."

Owen Campbell, publican
Murrisk, County Mayo

Map of Ireland showing wells cited in the text.

Map prepared by Shams Mortier.

Wells Cited in the Text and Located on the Map

Wells are numbered by order of their appearance in the text.

1. Knock Well, Knock, Co. Mayo
2. Eye well, Burren, Co. Clare
3. Tobar Pádraig, Kilmoremoy, Co. Mayo
4. Tobar Pádraig, Kiltormer, Co. Galway
5. Tobar Pádraic, Mám Éan, Co. Galway
6. Tobar Patráic, Ardmulchan, Co. Meath
7. St. Patrick's, Abby, Co. Donegal
8. St. Patrick's, Knockderc, Co. Limerick
9. St. Patrick's, Altadavin, Co. Tyrone
10. Well of the Wethers (Tobar na Molt, St. Patrick's well), Ardfert, Co. Kerry
11. Tobernault, Sligo, Co. Sligo
12. Tober Oglalla, Tulsk, Co. Roscommon
13. St. Dahlin's (St. Bridget's), Ballyheige, Co. Kerry
14. Tobar Faoi Fola (Tobar Alt na Peiste), Cnoc Fola, Co. Donegal
15. St. Lassair's Well, Lough Meelagh, Co. Roscommon
16. St. Brigid's Well, Cliffony, Co. Sligo
17. St. Molua's Well, Skirt, Co. Leix
18. Tullaghan Well, Tullaghan, Co. Sligo
19. St. Peakaun's Well, Glen of Aherlow, Co. Tipperary
20. St. John's Well, Dingle, Co. Kerry
21. St. Cronan's Well (Tobar Muire), Balla, Co. Mayo
22. Tooth Well, Burren, Co. Clare
23. St. Erc's Well, Listowel, Corridan Compound, Kerry Head, Co. Kerry
24. Children's Well, Malin Head, Co. Donegal
25. St. Eoin's Well, Listowel, Co. Kerry
26. St. Fechin's Well, Omey Island, Co. Galway
27. St. John's Well, Drumcullen Abbey, Co. Offaly
28. St. Brigid's Well, Armagh Demesne, Co. Armagh
29. Sunday's Well and Mary's Well, Walshestown, Co. Cork
30. Doon Well (Tobar an Duin), Kilmacrennan, Co. Donegal
31. St. Colman's Well, Gort, Co. Galway
32. St. Patrick's Well, Ballyshannon, Co. Donegal
33. St. Caillin's Well, Ballyconneely, Co. Galway
34. Lady Well, Abbey, Co. Galway
35. Seir Kieran, Clareen, Co. Offaly
36. St. Fechin's Well, Fore, Co. Westmeath
37. St. Ciaran's Well, Clonmacnoise, Co. Offaly
38. St. Olan's Well, Aghbullogue, Co. Cork
39. St. Attracta's Well, Monasteraden, Co. Roscommon
40. St. Declan's Well, Ardmore, Co. Waterford
41. Earl's Well, Kildare, Co. Kildare
42. Magh Adhair, Quin, Co. Clare
43. St. Molaisse's Well, Devinish Island, Co. Fermanagh
44. St. Patrick's Well and Bed, Maumeen, Co. Galway
45. St. Brigid's Well, Liscannor, Co. Clare
46. St. Michael's Well, Balleymore West, Co. Kerry
47. St. Patrick's Well, Dromard, Co. Sligo
48. St. Patrick's Well, Aughris, Co. Sligo
49. St. Margaret's Well, Ennis/Kilrush Road, Co. Clare

Crossing the Circle at

the Holy Wells of Ireland

Introduction

What's in a Name?

DURING A SPAN of fifteen years from 1979 to 1994 we have visited, measured, photographed, mapped, and tasted approximately five hundred Irish holy wells and have talked with both scholars and folk regarding the heritage of the particular sites. We remember fondly conversations with such people as Máire MacNeill, Hubert Butler, and Michael Herity. We have surveyed the literature, much of it written before this century, working back into the twilight mist of Irish oral mythology. Most important, we have felt the power at these places, from the much-publicized, papal-visited international site at Knock (well no. 1 on the map) to the tiny rabbit warren "eye well" on the Burren (2), hidden even from mapmakers. We would like to share our exploration of these places and their meanings, from the mythology and rituals surrounding the springs in pre-Christian Ireland to the coming of St. Patrick and the subsequent inversion of power as it is currently experienced at these Irish wells.

When we initially became interested in the project of the holy wells of Ireland, we ran into at least two confusing factors. Both had to do with the naming of the wells. Many wells have the same name regardless of location, and a single well may have several names. In addition, the designation of a particular saint's name may vary from well to well; for example, St. Bridget is patron of St. Bride's Well, Kilbride, County Mayo, St. Briget's Well, Kildare,

Eye well, Burren, Co. Clare (2). Paddy Nolan, a local
farmer, showed us this eye well. Statue, coins, and cup
attest to its continuing healing efficacy.

County Kildare, and St. Brigid's Well, Liscannor, County Clare. Further, the name Bridget may vary in spelling from place to place. In one area it may be spelled Brigit, in another Brigid, in still another Bridghet. This variation in spelling extends to other words in Irish as well. Thus, there is no universal spelling norm, at least in the countryside among the folk, but rather a regional standard. We have tried to remain true to these regional standards in order to maintain the local character of the sites.

On our very first trip to Ireland we were in pursuit of a certain well site in County Limerick. We stopped at the local pub to inquire as to its whereabouts. Several gentlemen gave what appeared to be conflicting directions concerning the location of the well. Yet all informants were adamant about the certainty of their facts. After investigating these leads, we realized that they were all correct and that we were being told about three different wells in the immediate neighborhood. To make the matter more confusing, all three wells were called St. Patrick's. Later we discovered that wells called St. Patrick's were distributed in plenty all over Ireland. To name a few, for example: Tobar Pádraig, Kilmoremoy, County Mayo (3); Tobar Pádraig, Kiltormer, County Galway (4); Tobar Pádraic, Mám Éan, County Galway (5); Tobar Patraic, Ardmulchan, County Meath (6); also St. Patrick's, Abby, County Donegal (7); St. Patrick's, Knockderc, County Limerick (8); St. Patrick's, Altadavin, County Tyrone (9). This list could go on and on and serves only to illustrate the problem we confronted in locating and identifying particular sites. In order to differentiate, it is crucial to know exactly where a well is located. Clearly, the place of the well is more important than the naming of it. However, it is also true that a different name does change the character of a well.

Another confusing factor about the wells for non-Irish speakers was apparent when we studied the ordinance survey maps and realized that a well could be varied in its generic naming. Not only could the phonetic designation for a watery healing place be different from region to region, but a single site might be referred to by several names. For example, we have *tober*, *tougher*, *tubber*, *tupper*, and *tipper*, to name a few. In addition, we found *seir*, *furran*, and *saighear*. These variations speak to the regional emphasis at the wells.

The difficulty of identifying the wells is also compounded by the fact that a single well may have several names or designations simultaneously. In the case of two of St. Patrick's wells in Ardfert, County Kerry (10), the original names were "Well of the Wethers" and "eye well." According to legend, Patrick circumambulated the whole of Ireland, "saining" or purifying wells, striking into the water with his staff, *Bachall Ísu*, and leaving a "flag" or flagstone to indicate that the well was now transformed from its pagan use into the service of Christianity. Tobernault in County Sligo (11) and Tober Oglalla in Tulsk, County Roscommon (12), are also often called St. Patrick's wells and provide further examples of this type of naming. Frequently accompanying the name changes were transformations of usage, such as the addition of stations of the cross to the more ancient ritual patterns of circumambulation that were practiced at wells in pre-Christian times.

Additional confusion at the wells has nothing to do with St. Patrick. For example, in Ballyheige, County Kerry, there is Tobar Súl, known also as St. Dahlin's and St. Bridget's (13). This well (*tobar*) is for eyes (*súil*) and is dedicated to two different saints. These three consecrations are obviously different.

The ultimate mercurial site is located at Cnoc Fola in County Donegal where a well called either Tobar Faoi Fola or Tobar Alt na Peiste (14) is found. But since it is covered by the sea at high tide, its visibility depends upon the time one visits there.

The changeability evident in the naming of wells is matched by the syncretism of the rituals performed at the site of the wells. We find wonderful amalgams employing cross-cultural and transhistorical ritual practices. Healing incantations, kingship rites, druidic rounds, and Catholic rites are being performed at a single site either serially or simultaneously. For instance, at St. Lassair's Well (15) a priest says Easter Mass upon a Celtic flagstone under which pilgrims will later crawl for the relief of back troubles. Rounds may be the stations of the cross or an *à soliel* pattern in imitation of the circuit of the pre-Christian king.

The water at these wells is changeable in many different ways. For instance, wells may pick up and move. St. Brigid's (Brideswell), Cliffony, County Sligo (16), and St. Molua's Well in Skirt, County Leix (17), are examples of moving wells. At Tullaghan Well (St. Patrick) in County Sligo (18), the water alternates salt and fresh. The lore tells us that the waters may be offended by such practices as the washing of clothes or the fencing off of the well. There are many such cases described in the Ordinance Survey Letters, Ordinance Survey Office, Phoenix Park, Dublin. One letter mentions two of the reasons that wells move, the washing of clothes and the barring of public access to the well. A description of St. Peakaun's Well, Glen of Aherlow, County Tipperary (19), notes: "Well is now just a shallow depression, ancient looking trees near it, in fields of dry flat rockland. . . . a patron was held on the last Sunday of July known locally as Garlic Sunday. Rounds were performed. The young people danced on the flagstones. Several tents were set up where punch and *poitín* were on sale. Matchmaking and courtship were a feature. The patron was put down by Father McKiernan of Cloone. The parson who lived nearby had the right of way to the well taken away. . . . The well moved twice, from the graveyard in Cloone to Esker T., where a woman washed clothes in it, and thence to its present site (one mile south of Cloone)."[1]

In addition to leaving when angered, it is said that wells may remain and be spiteful, causing dire consequences to persons or their possessions. When a farmer tried diverting St. John's Well (a lady's well) in Dingle, County Kerry (20), cattle got sick and some even died. When he stopped this practice, the sick cows recovered. Another man is said to have put up a fence at St. John's Well where people did rounds. Because he prevented this practice, all his animals died.[2]

In yet another kind of change, wells simply lose power, as we find at St. Cronan's Well in Balla, County Mayo (21), where all is overgrown and forgotten, in weeds and ruin, and the town, which was a thriving pilgrimage site in the 1840s, was until recently desolate and unused. Some of our informants said, "Now, everyone goes to Knock." Balla was first associated with St. Cronan. Lame and despised by his parents, he was raised by St. Comgal in Bangor. When he left St. Comgal, he asked for a token to show where he might establish his own church. He was given a fountain that had preceded him as a shining cloud. When he reached a certain place, the cloud vanished and reappeared as a well surrounded by a wall, a wall so beautiful that the place was named Balla, meaning "wall."[3] Other lore concerning Balla tells of Patrick ringing his bell and striking his staff into the ground; when he pulled up his staff, the well appeared.

August 15 was the important day of pilgrimage, with many pilgrims going round the cemetery on their knees saying fifteen decades of the rosary in the night. At daybreak they continued on their knees toward the well, circling

St. Cronan's Well (Tobar Muire), Balla, Co. Mayo (21).
Ruined site at Balla that is being restored in 1994.

two mounds near the well three times. Then the waters were applied, and it was believed that any ailment could be cured, especially of the eyes. An indentation from St. Cronan's elbow in a stone next to the well collected water that was applied to the eyes for this cure. Cattle were also taken to the river at this site for healing, and butter was thrown into the water as an offering. In former years, on August 14, young girls dressed in white would process to the site and place a flower garland on the statue of Mary. But now, according to our informant, the children are unwilling to participate. This well is sometimes called Tobar Muire (well of our Lady) as well as its more common name, St. Cronan.

One final story about this well may relate to its demise. In the seventeenth century there was a large estate owned by a Protestant English family. The well and the chapel, which once stood at the edge of this estate, were reached by a gate through which the Catholic servants would go to attend Mass. The Protestant owners had the gate closed up with several large stones. Given what we have described about the "personality" of wells, perhaps this act was the beginning of the decline of power at Balla.

We discovered also in our journeys a group of wells retaining much of their pre-Christian character. Far out on the Burren in County Clare lies a tiny well known as the "Tooth Well" (22). It has never been given the name of a Christian saint. On a windswept rocky area of the southwest far from any village are found many standing stone circles and ancient roadways. No buildings are in sight, although here and there a few cattle pick a living from between the stones. One could come within a few feet of this spring and overlook it. We spent a good deal of time looking for it by fanning out and searching the ground. We finally spotted it, more by intuitive grace than by the directions of Paddy Nolan, a local farmer.

Lodged at the center of two concentric stone circles is a beautiful azure blue pool scarcely six inches across, lying under a miniature stone table. Votives found here consist of human teeth, bones, and stones, and occasionally a picked wild daffodil. This well is active, but visitors come individually rather than in groups. The cures are for toothache and arthritis. This well displays little evidence of Christian presence; nevertheless, it continues in its function as a healing site among the folk at the present time. Christianity is not, therefore, necessary for the survival of the ancient sites.

Another well that may be said not to depend upon Christianity for viability is the Corridan family well on Kerry Head, County Kerry (23). A last

Tooth Well, Burren, Co. Clare (22). Ancient and sparsely
Christianized well that is still active for cures of teeth and
bones.

example to mention is the Children's Well in Malin, County Donegal (24), which is revealed only at low tide. Part of a group of three underwater wells, the Children's Well can be distinguished from the other two (if you can find them) because it puts forth "oily" water. Whooping cough and other throat and chest maladies are said to give way to the power of this water.

These contemporary examples from our files of wells with little Christian influence reveal that the foundation of the power of venerated springs lies in the mutability of water and in its earthy source. Christianity accepted this power, despite its apparent difference from the Celtic goddess-centered tradition. It now remains to determine how such a syncretism could be possible. The many-sided nature of these wells presented tremendous difficulties for the interpretation of their significance. In an effort to accommodate this multiplicity without recognizing some features and ignoring others, we have used the following phenomenological method.

Methodological Prologue

The reenactment of myths and rituals at these holy wells that we are about to describe seems worthy of serious consideration by the phenomenologist of religion. The approach we take in this study is one that considers both the general symbolic and ahistorical dimension of the venerated spring and the particular Irish historical context in which these springs are found. In using such an approach, we have tried to remain sensitive to our own intuitions and to the symbolic insights of others, while at the same time using systematic and analytic tools in the gathering and compilation of the Irish historical material. It is our goal not simply to document the phenomenon of the Irish holy well[4] but to understand the nature and particular "intentionality" (see chapter 4) of those wells within the broad framework of human religiousness and within the peculiar context of Celtic Irish culture. Our method therefore has a dual focus. We are seeking at the same time an understanding of the universal or timeless aspects of venerated springs that might be found throughout the history of religions and an understanding of those uniquely Irish aspects that both add to and blend with the universal symbolism of the springs. When these focuses are combined, we believe that the result is a broader, deeper, and more precise understanding of venerated springs, an understanding that is more complete and more holistic than would otherwise be possible.

We would characterize ourselves broadly as phenomenologists of religion. In keeping with that tradition, we make no claim to being specialists in Celtic or Irish studies. We feel that whatever contribution we make comes not from the gathering and classifying of new material but from the interpretation of that material which may lead to a deeper and more meaningful understanding of these holy wells.

When we refer to the religiousness of humankind or to the sacred as a quality we seek to understand, it must be kept in mind that such abstract notions are meaningful only in their historical expressions. In other words, the religiousness of humankind that we seek to understand always presents itself through history. History in the phenomenological sense takes two primary forms. First are those forms that are psychic in nature, that is, they do not appear in material form—for example, dreams. Second, history may be manifest in forms that are somatic or material in their expression—for example, sporting events. Within the sphere of religious history, these two fundamental ways of expression are termed myth (psychic) and ritual (somatic).[5] These two structures are found in all religious expressions in varying proportions. Sometimes one will dominate the other, but on rare occasions they will be in balance. For example, within the two basic forms of Christianity, Catholicism and Protestantism, myth and ritual have very different proportional values. Within the Protestant tradition the word, which is a mythic form, is intentionally dominant over ritual, while in the Catholic tradition with its emphasis upon the Mass and sacraments, ritual plays a more important role. In some cases the ritual that at one time accompanied the myth is forgotten, while in other cases an act may be performed for which the meaning of the myth is lost. By intention, however, religious appearances always contain both forms.

Before moving directly into myth and ritual and their connection with Irish venerated springs, we need to make a further methodological distinction. In addition to the fact that all religious phenomena intend both mythic and ritualistic forms, religious worlds themselves are manifest historically in two fundamental or archetypal ways in consonance with their ecological origin and development. Those religious worlds or cultures that developed in areas suitable for hunting or herding engender religious forms whose power source is found in the sky or heavens. Such religions as Zoroastrianism, Islam, and Judaism were all developed in arid or semiarid settings that, in their vastness and openness, symbolically reflect the sky, a sky where the single sovereign god dwells. All power and all creative impulses come from this sky sovereign. This same symbolism prevails in tribal cultures with similar arid ecological situations, such as those of various African herders as well as Siberian and Indo-European tribal peoples whose culture is centered on animals. Religious symbolism within these worlds tends to emphasize the power of a male sky-god who imposes his will upon a world created by him and who creates as well as intervenes in history. Following Mircea Eliade, we choose to call these religions historical.[6]

The second fundamental religious form, and the one with which we are chiefly concerned here, is linked to an ecological milieu that abounds in fertility. Fertility is the central symbol of power and is derived primarily from the earth. The most important secondary symbol that gives evidence of the power of the earth is the plant. In contrast to the historical animal-centered cultures whose single sovereign sky-god is male, the power of fertility in the plant-centered cultures is manifest in multiple female goddesses. The earth itself is often imaged as *magna mater,* and this motherly imagery is repeated on different scales throughout the culture. It is found in the plant, in the moon, in water, and in women. The primary religious event that is derived from this fecundating power is that of death and rebirth, or rejuvenation. This primary event is observed in the seasonal death and rebirth of plants, in the phases of the moon, in the coming and going of the tides, and in the menstrual cycle of women.[7] Thus, within the human realm it is female rather than male who is the source of religious power, and she wields that power through her ability to create in material form. We choose to call these religious forms cosmic.

The impetus toward cyclic regeneration in earth-centered cultures brings with it a resistance toward change or evolution. On the one hand, the sky-oriented or historical culture sees its salvation coming by moving through a linear time sequence that continually improves in quality until it reaches its ultimate goal. On the other hand, the earth or cosmic culture achieves religious power through the repetition of creative events in a circle of time that is self-renewing. These repetitions take the form of rituals that recur periodically, often associated with seasonal change, resulting in the re-creation of the world. This world re-creation is achieved through the repetition of the same events that occurred at the beginning of the world, based on the assumption that, because of structural correlation, the repetition of that original event is that event in a renewed form. The form, then, is both ancient and contemporary.

There is a myth from the Indonesian island of Ceram that tells how the world was danced into form by the nine tribes of humankind through their sacrifice of the maiden Hainuwele. From her body came the banana, from which the nine tribes are descended, as are the pigs, porcelain dishes, Chinese gongs, and all things that have power and make life what it is. This is a cosmogonic event, and Hainuwele's dance is performed seasonally without fail, thus repeating the original creation and through its repetition renewing the world. Here we see the religious importance of circles (the dance takes on a spiral form); of plants (the bananas), which give life and are one in substance with humankind; and of woman, from whose body comes life in its many forms.[8]

Religious worlds, then, in their two primary forms of the historical and the cosmic, present two major contexts in which the more universal symbols such as those of the sacred spring are worked out and amplified. Many springs are considered to be sacred in both historical and cosmic ecologies, but the interpretation of their symbolism from one to the other can be quite different.

1

The Nature of the Sacred Spring

Echoes of the Past

AN IRISH MAIDEN, on the eve of her wedding, peers into a spring and sees a golden trout, which she describes as "a saint, perhaps." An arthritic old man carefully and painfully eases himself lengthwise under a large flagstone or table stone that is raised a few inches above the damp earth beside a spring. Women place egg-shaped stones picked up on the beach at a tiny spring by the sea. Some combs, pins, a cane, and other personal items lay in a crypt surrounding a spring on a hill. A swastika-shaped St. Bridget's cross constructed of fresh green sweet grass floats on a cress-covered spring. These are accounts not of ancient and historical incidents, as one might suppose, but rather of current living rituals occurring at the present time near certain Irish springs, now known as holy wells. These activities, in some cases, are found in continuity from prehistoric times to the present.[1]

Our bride, Mrs. Mary Costello, now eighty years old, of Ardee, Listowel, County Kerry, tells us that she had no specific wish when she visited St. Eoin's Well (25), but that she has lived "without too much trouble" and has "recovered every time from spells" (ailments, evidently severe). She told her experiences to another Ardee well-goer and found hers to be identical. Ellen Walsh was quite crippled and went to the well to drink for a cure. She also did the prescribed rounds or patterns and saw a trout in the well. She was cured and, although left with a permanent limp, managed very well thereaf-ter. Martin Mulvihill, also of Ardee, verifies the women's stories.

The trout that the women saw was golden, about ten inches long. It leaped from the bank at the entrance of the well about ten feet to the upper end of the well and disappeared. The water percolated furiously—evidence of *na bolcca immaiss,* or bubbles of inspiration, as were found at the mythical Well of Segais.[2] Mrs. Costello also told us how the well had moved from "east of the bridge" after people living in Snugborough had washed clothes in the spring. Amergin, chief bard of the Milesians (who were the last of the five mythic invaders, and are generally considered to be the Celts), speaks out of the twilight alphabet calendar: "I am a salmon in a pool. . . ."[3]

More living rituals take place at St. Laisser's Well near Lough Meelagh, between Keadue and Ballyfarnan, County Roscommon. The well is situated next to a sacred tree encrusted with old and new coins, "clooties" (or frag-ments of cloth), and rosaries. There are healing features at this site: the water of the well, blessed clay balls greatly treasured as guardians of the home, and a huge capstone, or table, under which back troubles are relieved. On a cer-tain day, August 15, Bishop Daley arrives at the site with a band, and commu-nity people march to the shrine from Keadue. A Mass is said, offerings are made to the tree, arthritics pass under the low table stone on their backs, and clay is gathered in marble-sized balls from across the road where the well was once situated. We have reminders from the twelfth-century "Vision of Mac Conglinne":

> We stretch ourselves
> Beneath the shield of thy might
> May some fruit of the tree of passion
> Fall on us this night![4]

Resting just above the high-tide mark on Omey Island, St. Fechin's Well (26) brings to mind a vagina. It is long and low, pointing toward the master ocean. The salt sea enters its sweet water at the high tide of the full moon. Women walk along the beach to this spring, bringing egg-shaped stone offerings with the hope of becoming pregnant. January 16 is an auspicious day here, according to Mr. Mannion, draper, of Clifden. A pattern consists of circumambulating the well seven times and depositing seven stones. Masses are also held here currently by the Clifden parish priest, Father Meraty, who says that St. Fechin came to this place and established a monastery in the sixth century. We also find a standing stone circle and two spiral beds in association, which indicate a pre-Christian site. In the *Leabhar Gabhála* we hear described those early women from the first invasion of Ireland, Noah's relations who were refused the refuge of the ark and later landed in Ireland with three men whom they literally killed with excessive sexual activity. Then,

> On a lonely headland the women assembled
> Chill as worshippers in a nave,
> And watched the eastern waters gather
> Into a great virile flooding wave.[5]

While scholars in anthropology and the history of religions do not generally examine these kinds of phenomena, exceptions to this neglect are demonstrated in a statement by Anne Ross that the wells and water cults are "the only religious phenomena in continuity."[6] Also, Mircea Eliade describes hydrological activities from the Neolithic to the present day. Both Neolithic and Roman ex-voto offerings have been found in the springs at Grisy, St. Sauveur, St. Moritz, Bertinoro, and St. Andeol, among other sites that remain active today.[7]

In addition to votive offerings, other practices that are ongoing at the springs include drinking the water for cures and grace; placing objects into the well; personifying wells that evolve from a cult god to the name of a saint; putting twigs, egg stones, or berries in or near the water; associating a flagstone or tree with a particular spring; and presenting for a cure the cloth fragments or clooties that signify disease.

The springs themselves continue to participate actively today by housing fish (usually trout or eels of great and indestructible power); assuming the burdens of various diseases (visual or mental troubles, and the like); creating a deluge or moving away when disturbed or desecrated; and turning red, oily, salty, or poisonous through various negative interactions with humans and gods.

The Nature of Sacred Water

In the beginning, to emphasize the importance of holy wells, it might be helpful to review the nature of water itself and its symbolism. Water is spoken of as the source, the healer, and the essence of plant life. The regenerative ability of water, its power to fertilize and bring about new birth, is the pattern of life itself: *aqua vita, ma* (the Sumerian word for conception).

The pattern of the tides, governed by the moon, is imitative of the cycles of the earth: sowing and harvesting, living and dying. The water, in itself, cannot be formed except as it gives itself to a stream, river, bog, pond, or well, coming as a flood, rainstorm, mist, or snow. It is known also by the tracks it leaves upon stone and earth where it has coursed repeatedly. We can know water only by its container or what it is surrounded by, and its form is as diverse as a dewdrop or a great flood. Thus water's shifting shape, determined by the form of containment, is found to have immense numinous power. The particular form of containment we are studying here is the spring or holy well, especially that of Ireland, where the essential nature of water is revealed so clearly.

This book shows how water itself is *fons et origo* (fountain and source), transformer, healer, and regenerative force. Its symbolic power transcends all powers, yet its form is never stable. Water that is contained, as in a well, lends a spiritual quality to certain places, and it is these places that have demanded attention from the very earliest human experience to the present. The symbol itself, water, is transformative, eternal, giver of life and meaning. Within the context of this eternality, however, there are numerous and varying forms; the ocean continues to undulate; and rain falls, nourishes the earth, and is carried back into the sky or rushes to join the great rivers passing downward to the mother ocean. Water is different and yet the same, as is the way in which we interpret its power as we explore its continuity throughout the ages.

On the level of cosmogonic symbolism, water facilitates life, which might float into being as a tree coming from a watery navel, be thrown up or vomited from the throat, or perhaps appear through the menstrual/urine flooding of a goddess.[8] The nature of sacred water is such that its power cannot be eliminated by fashion, dogma, or decree, but rather its interpretation must be redefined. Thus the use of water and its archetypal functions do not disappear but instead underlie historically specific rituals and practices germane to particular sites. Even complete inundation results in something, such as the hidden city that dwells beneath Lake Carman in County Wexford.[9]

For example, St. Patrick "sained," or purified, many wells in his journeys around Ireland, thus rescuing those wells from pagan practices and putting them in the service of the Catholic church. In order to include well worship within the sky-god context of Christianity, it was necessary for St. Patrick to purify these wells, thus converting the power found at these places to the service of his church. There were some interesting moments of transition for St. Patrick as he attempted to incorporate the pagan cult of immersion with the "purity" of death as a means of "sight."

Persistence and Continuity in the Use of Sacred Springs

In determining the links between the prehistoric and modern use of holy wells, we find several clues. Much evidence lies in the archaeology of the votive offerings found in the wells. Hieroglyphs representing spiral, snail, fish, and woman are found at wells presently in use. These depictions have existed since Neolithic times. People still offer gifts to the wells and incorporate ancient objects into ritual practices or "patterns" or rounds performed near the wells. These objects may be touched, incised, rubbed, sat upon, or otherwise used in a ritual, following a strict set of orders, which if violated would destroy the whole effect or even bring about a disaster. Other objects attesting to the antiquity of well sites are cauldrons, bronze decorative strips, chalices, stone beds, flags, patterns, and spiral walkways still revered as part of a ritual whole.

A most interesting example of the persistence and continuity of water symbolism may be found in the association of pins and water. In the Irish tale of *Balor's Raid on McKinnelly's Cow*,[10] a rather complex myth, we are concerned with one particular motif: the attempt of a threatened sovereign to do away with triplet baby gods who are pinned in a cloth for drowning. The pin comes undone, and one babe manages to slip out of the binding. His survival, through the releasing action of the pin, facilitates the rest of the action in the tale: that is, that the child is destined to slay his grandfather, the *senex*, and become the young ruler, thus fulfilling the Celtic process of renewal through water and the pin. The place where this occurred is now known as the Bay of the Pin. This place-name gives importance to the dynamic of the water and the pin, rather than to the grandson per se. Water and pin both participate in enclosing and securing yet when loosened, bring forth the means of regeneration, a symbolic "giving." A pin or brooch given to the water in the well facilitates the freeing of power at that place. The putting together of pins and water symbolically encourages the releasing of regenerative forces today, in continuity with the Balor theme. Current offerings of pins may be found at many well sites today. An example of a "pin well," as they are called, is St. John's Well, Drumcullen Abbey, County Offaly (27), where pins and brooches are scattered near the well and rock, especially on St. John's Eve.

Another example of the persistence of ritual activity at the holy well is found at the "eye wells." There are many wells where people bathe their eyes. This ritual has arisen in legends such as the *Eddas*, when Odin gave his eye for a drink of the wisdom-giving well of Mimir. In Ireland at many sites we find a legend in which Brigit plucks out and gives her eyes to an admirer and then restores her "sight" or wisdom by bathing her orbits in a well.[11] One such example is St. Brigid's Well (28) at Armagh Demesne.

Near other eye wells we hear fragments of the theme from the *Adventures of Nera*, an epic of early Irish origin. Part of the action involves a blind man carrying a lame man to a well near Cruachen, on behalf of King Brion. The blind man asks, "Is it there?" and the lame man says, "It is." "It" is the king's golden crown, safe in the well, where wisdom or sovereignty dwells.

Eye wells are thus more important for the purpose of gaining wisdom or inner grace through "seeing" than merely for the cure of sore eyes irritated by peat smoke. The reduction of this inner sight to a cure for sore eyes did not include the total loss of meaning, as much lore about blind men carried on horses, lame horses, and various versions of the lame and the blind still abounds.

Circumambulation, a common activity today at the wells, is another example of the continuity of ritual practice. Quite structured patterns, or patrons, or rounds are still done. For example, at St. John's Well in Dingle (Tobar Eoin), rounds currently include three circuits at the well repeated nine times, with pebbles used to count the rounds. Afterwards one goes up the hill around a field and then back down to the well. There is trouble there now because the owners of the field do not want people up there, and the well is going dry and falling into disrepair.

The directive to travel *à soliel*, or in a sunwise or clockwise direction, follows the early pattern of kingship as found in the king's circuit about Ireland gathering hostages, in which the sea was at the royal left shoulder. Any variation in direction such as circling to the left would be considered sinister rather than adroit (to the right) and would violate a *geis* (taboo) of the king, bringing disaster upon the crops or a blight upon the land. The penalty for the king would be loss of life and fertility. The present-day patterns must be performed correctly as well, and all agree that it is better not to do anything around the well than to perform in the wrong direction. There are wells that have cursed those who have erred and have brought financial misfortune or illness to those who did not follow the ritual correctly. Patterns are specific ritual body movements and prayers, directions for which may often be found carved or printed at a well site to aid the pilgrim in the correct behavior.

One final example that demonstrates the antiquity and continuity of well-site activity is the practice of imbibing. Cups for drinking are found at most active wells, even if people also bathe there. The well is seen as an archetypal vessel of plenty, a constant source of all that water has to offer: wisdom, healing, inspiration, fertility, and regeneration. The Christian practices today at the wells may involve such activities as praying the stations of the cross in imitation or incorporation of the patterns, but the participants do not necessarily use the old paths. Pilgrims may both do the stations of the cross and perform the ancient patterns. Water that is holy to the church (such as that found in the baptismal font) is never imbibed; we may find a Catholic Mass performed at a holy well, but the drinking of water is not a part of that ritual. Following the Mass, however, water from the well may be drunk.

"And none will have knowledge who drinks not a draught out of the well."
Manannan mac Lir[12]

The existence of holy wells today provides a rare opportunity in the history of religions to witness sacred sites and rituals that have continued in form and use from prehistoric times to the present. Because of this established continuity with prehistory, we are able today both to study and practice rituals and to examine firsthand sites that may be as ancient as the Pyramids.

We hope to make a start in this book toward consolidating data on these wells and to begin the interpretative task central to the phenomenologist of religion. The particular form of containment for the water found in the wells manifests a type of power that has long moved humankind. We are also cognizant of the importance of the phenomenon of origin or source in this persistence of power. Finally, we feel that water itself has been and will remain a central talisman in the psyche of humankind because of its transformative and regenerative power. We hope that what is presented here will stimulate others to continue and expand the search into the meaning of the sacred spring and to use those springs of ancient wisdom in this search.

2

Myth and Ritual
at Celtic Irish Springs

The Celts and Cosmic Symbolism

THE CELTS, who had such a strong religious influence on the native Irish, participated in what we have referred to earlier as a cosmic worldview or religious system. In such a worldview, power is found primarily in the configurations of the cosmos, especially those of the earth. In the natural realm such things as trees, stones, caves, and various water formations, including the spring, are containers of great sacred power. In the human sphere women are the primary power bearers, and the mysteries of birth, death, and rebirth present in their bodily rhythms and activities are reflected in the phases of the moon, the tides of the sea, and the death and rebirth of plants.

The Celts in Ireland, of course, brought variations and emphases to the general cosmic pattern that both set them apart and enhanced or amplified the symbolism. They were a sedentary grain-cultivating and cattle-raising people who, although possessing a warrior aristocracy, were dependent upon the earth (identified as a goddess with various names) for their daily bread and for the wisdom and sovereignty to rule the land.[1] In the Irish case there is no single myth that can hold claim to being the definitive myth of creation, but in several instances, and on differing scales, we find that creation took place through a flooding of the world from which emerged the new land.[2] The land was then furnished through a series of events that established places such as rivers, plains, and mountains, until the formation of the world was completed.[3]

Thus, water and its symbolism played a central role as a creative force in the cosmic religiousness of the Irish Celts. Earlier we referred more generally to the symbolic power of water, that is, to its psychic or mythic aspects. In Irish mythology water was seen as a regenerative force. One either drank or circumambulated it ritually or was immersed ritually within it. These rites were regenerative as they took place at the critical times of seasonal transition. We suspect that these rites also were central to the rite of inauguration of kings that ritualized the periodic renewal of the earth as divine mother and queen of the king.

A second prominent feature of Irish Celtic cosmogony is the power of place. Recall that it was through a flood that the places of Ireland were made possible, and that these places were created by the events that occurred there. Thus Ireland was created over a period of time and was brought into being by water and made up of places. What is important more generally here is that in most cosmic or earth-centered religions, the places on the earth possess a particular power that is creative and regenerative. This is certainly true in Ireland, and this power of place is an essential element of the power and sacredness of the holy well.

We have earlier referred to the importance of the container of the water as an influence on the form of power present in the water. For example, a river has a different form of power than a spring. The former has a linear quality that informs the general symbolic character of the water, and the latter a circular quality as informant of the water symbolism. In other words, the context in which the water is found influences the particular nature of its power or sacrality. It is this context or situation as it is found on the earth's surface that we define as "place." The shape of the earth's surface creates innumerable nooks and crannies, each having a different quality about it and thus defining itself as a place having its own particular power. The world, then, is made up of many places, each one self-contained and self-generating.

The ancient Irish countryside was dotted with such places, each of which emanated a particular feeling or power. It was this power arising from the place that made possible the events that actually named each place. Battles were staged at fords because fords are a place of crossing and transformation or change. The battle or duel brought on such change in the human world, and the ford was thus named for this transformation. Human activity was generally in harmony with the place, and thus the name that arose truly thematized the nature of the place. Entire texts in Irish literature, such as *The Metrical Dindshenchas*,[4] are devoted to descriptions of the nature of a place and how that nature came to be. Thus, the names that arose from these etiological myths described both the event that caused the name and the nature of the place, which was contained in the name. For this reason place-names are extremely important in Ireland because place is important, and place is important because it is a part of the earth who is a goddess and mother of the people.

Corresponding to the nature of a place were the people who dwelt there. They were connected ontologically to the place and carried a name that was often associated with it. Their connection to the place was cemented by the fact that they were born there, that they emerged, as it were, from that place. Thus they were children of the spirit or deity of the place. The head of their family, their chief, was the consort of this deity. As Proinsias Mac Cana states, "The sacral king is the spouse of his kingdom and his inauguration ceremony is known as *banais righi*, 'wedding feast of kingship'; in other words he is then ritually united with the sovereignty of the territory over which he rules."[5]

There is a tradition still recounted in County Clare in a section called the Burren. The Burren is a large ridge of limestone that rises steeply from the sea between the small villages of Ballyvaughan and Corofin. It is highly charged with the power of place, and one can find many sacred monuments and forts left there by Celtic and pre-Celtic peoples. What is so remarkable is that this extremely stony area not only supports some exotic flora but also provides some of the best grazing feed for cattle in Ireland. The reason for both these anomalies is that the limestone holds a tremendous amount of heat, and thus grass and flowers not native to Ireland thrive year round. Just beyond the Burren, on the edge of the sea, the rock changes and is not so porous; thus, it does not hold the heat. It is "cold stone." Now Ballyvaughan lies beside the sea in the cold stone area, and Corofin lies on the edge of the Burren inland. The tradition states that cold stone will never meet warm stone, which practically translates into a prohibition against intermarriage between the people of the two areas. Thus, the people of Ballyvaughan and Corofin were identified with the place in their nature and because of their nativity.

The connection we see between the place of birth and the people dwelling there amounts to a connection between body and earth. That is, body and earth are of the same substance. The place, or the earth, is the mother of the people. In Ireland this is called a *tuath,* which means both the place where the people live and the people themselves.[6] This connection or identity between place and family is viewed as sacred. Thus, as a hierophany, or expression of the sacred, it falls in one of the two primary forms of religious manifestation. In this case we are dealing with a somatic or physical phenomenon, so the importance of place finds itself in the general category of ritual. In fact, rituals in Celtic Ireland were enacted by the body and were focused on a place, usually the center of the *tuath,* which was the place both of creation and of death in that the chief was inaugurated there and buried there. The physical form of this center was that of a mound. It was both the shape and the location of the mound that provided its power. Interestingly, the power of the mound lay within it, that is, in its interior rather than on top of it. Nearby was located, as part of the center complex, a sacred tree, or *bile,* a sacred stone, and a holy well.

In summary, we find that the sacred always expresses itself through some thing or event that we term history. Also, these religious expressions tend to take two primary forms, based upon the geographical context in which the hierophany occurs. These forms we earlier termed historical and cosmic. In the case of Celtic Ireland, we are engaged with a cosmic religious form whose primary power comes from the earth imaged as a goddess. There are some historical factors to consider, however, since a male warrior aristocracy existed, and much value was placed upon cattle.[7] Despite this variation, power and creativity derive from the feminine images as goddess, earth/place, or woman/cow.

Myth and the Celtic Springs

We have thus far suggested that myth in a religious context is psychic in form and is accompanied by ritual, which is somatic in form. Also we have found that both phenomena occur in both major forms of religion, that is, cosmic and historical. We have not mentioned, however, what myths do or the nature of their content.

To begin with, myths contain within them the first forms or archetypes of all creative action. In other words, they provide humankind with models for living, models that, because they were established at the beginning of time by the gods, are eternal in duration and unchanging in nature. In addition, myths contain a supernatural quality because they are established by supernatural beings who perform feats of supernatural character in a world that transcends natural law. This mythic quality is transmitted partly by the events or history of the narrative and partly by the form of language used.[8]

Because myths establish models for all significant creative action, they establish a world, a coherent whole in which humans dwell together in relationship to the sacred. Thus, it is the cosmogonic myth that is primary over all other myths and that sets the way of being and the sources of power within the world.

Now we wish to apply this understanding of myth to our study of Irish sacred springs. What is it myths tell us symbolically about these sacred springs that we can use in arriving at an understanding of the ancient use of the springs and of why use of the springs has continued uninterrupted into present times?

When we survey Irish myths that contain references to sacred springs, we find there is one myth that is foundational for the others and establishes the models upon which other instances of sacred springs are grounded. This myth also tells us a lot about the religious function, power, and nature of the Irish sacred spring.

The myth to which we refer describes a sacred spring located in what the ancient Irish called the Otherworld. Before relating this description, it is important that one have an understanding of the nature of the Otherworld and its religious significance. The Otherworld is a place in the special sense of that word that we have been using. In fact, it is the most sacred of places and contains more power than any other object, person, or place. Still further, it is the source of all power and sacrality including that which is located in the ordinary world. Thus, it plays the mythic role of establishing archetypes or models for powerful actions and events, objects, and people. It would correspond functionally to the Judeo-Christian paradise or heaven, but it does contain some very different meanings. Some names for the Otherworld give us a sense of its ambivalent nature: The Terrible Valley, The Land of Promise, The Green Isle, The Lonesome Isle, The Land under the Wave, The

Plains of Delight, and The Land of Ever-Living Women. Specifically, the Otherworld is both the land of the dead and the land of eternal youth. Further, it is of a feminine nature and is often thought of as inhabited only by women or ruled by women. Its location(s) gives us further clues to its essence. It is variously under the earth, within a mound, under the sea, in the far west on an island, and in the far east on a plain hidden in mist.

In sum, the Otherworld is the source of power, fecundity, and wisdom, all of which must be thought of as differing aspects of the same thing. It is an essentially feminine power and is identified with the earth, that is, with Ireland. As a source of all power, it establishes the power structures that are present on the surface world. Thus, the surface world is a reflection of the Otherworld. In fact, access between these worlds is possible at special times of the year. In keeping with its feminine nature, the wisdom that is central to Otherworld power is intuitive and focuses on an understanding of "the way things are" as well as the foretelling of the future or, more succinctly put, of the workings of fate.

Contained in the Otherworld are four talismans that bear power beyond comprehension and that are models for corresponding objects on the surface world. They are the Great Fál, a sacred stone that screams aloud when the future king of Ireland touches it; the spear of Lug, which never misses its mark; the sword of Nuadu, from which no one escapes; and the cauldron of the Dagda, which no one can empty of food.[9] Essential to all of these talismans are fecundity and wisdom or, rather, the wisdom of fecundity.

Now we come to what is for us the most important content of the Otherworld. At the center of the Otherworld and surrounded by the four talismans is located the miraculous Well of Segais. This is a sacred spring and is characterized in several texts as the source of all wisdom that is contained in its waters and the source of the most sacred rivers in Ireland, the Boyne and the Shannon.[10] Surrounding the well are nine hazel trees. The trees drop their red berries into the well. In one variant the berries flow from the well into the rivers Shannon and Boyne. If one finds them and eats them, one gains of the wisdom of the goddess. The other variant of the myth states that in the well dwells a marvelous salmon known as the salmon of wisdom, or *eo fis*. The salmon eats the berries, and they cause his red spots. Whoever catches and eats the salmon will gain the occult wisdom of "the way things are." Finally, when the hazel berries drop into the well, they cause bubbles to rise, which themselves are evidence of the living force and the presence of wisdom in the water. These bubbles are called in Irish *na bolcca immaiss,* the bubbles of mystic inspiration that we described in chapter 1 when the woman came to the well of St. Eoin on her wedding night.

There are several other myths that extend and amplify the myth of the Well of Segais and that we consider to be the germinal myth for the hierophany of the holy well. The most important of these for our purposes concerns Finn mac Cumaill, central character in one of the main bodies of Irish literature, known as the Fianna Cycle.[11] Finn himself was a manifestation of the surface god, son or grandson of the Otherworld god, who seeks the wisdom and the wife of his father/grandfather. This woman is the Great Goddess. In this quest he often crosses the boundary between the surface world and the Otherworld, returning to the surface world, if successful, with wisdom and sovereignty. In order to gain this wisdom, he must kill the Otherworld lord with his own weapon, the magical spear of Lug being an example, and marry the Otherworld queen, his own mother. This mythic process repeats itself over and over again in Irish myth within the different cycles.

In the myth of how Finn gained this wisdom of the Otherworld, we see that it was gained by drinking from the Well of Segais in various ways. There are three versions of the myth all lodged in a prose tale called in Irish *Feis Tighe Conáin,* or "Feast of Conán's House," which itself is within the Fianna Cycle. One day Finn and two friends were on the top of a *síd* (mound)[12] named Carn Feradaig. They found that the door to the *síd* was ajar, and they tried to go in. But the daughters of Bec mac Buain, lord of the *síd* and thus of the Otherworld as well, closed the door on them. In the struggle some water from the sacred well, held in a pitcher by one of the daughters, spilled on the lips of Finn and his friends. At that moment they acquired *fios,* or wisdom.[13] A variant of this myth, found in another tale within the same cycle, recounts the same situation but at a different location. Finn and two friends are on top of Carn Coirrshleibhe, another *síd,* and are about to enter the door. The three daughters of Bec mac Buain each hold a pitcher in their hand containing water from the sacred well. They slam the door on Finn, and in the commotion they spill water from the pitcher onto his thumb, which is caught in the door. Finn pulls his thumb from the door and immediately puts it into his mouth to ease the pain. When he does, he swallows some of the sacred water and is given wisdom at once.

One more of the Fianna accounts is worth mentioning because it raises another theme that often accompanies the well mythos. This is the theme of the fish in the well. The fish is a magic one and always some form of anadromoid; we have seen instances of both salmon and eels. Patrick Logan gives an instance of two adjoining wells in Walshestown, County Cork, called Sunday's Well and Mary's Well (29). In one of the wells, Mary's Well, there was a trout. In Sunday's Well there was an eel. In every case the fish is the bearer and bringer of wisdom.

To return to the Finnian myth, Finn as a young man goes to study poetry with a teacher, Finn Eces, who dwelt by the sacred river Boyne. It was said that Finn Eces would one day catch the magic salmon living in the pool of Linn Feic, and that from the moment of eating him he would attain complete wisdom. Indeed, he did catch the magic salmon, and he gave it to Finn to cook for him. While cooking the fish, Finn accidentally touched the salmon and burned his thumb. He immediately put his thumb in his mouth to cool it. His teacher saw him and acknowledged him as a man possessing the magical wisdom. Finn was then given the salmon to eat.

There is yet another dimension of the wisdom derived from the well. This is the connection of wisdom with sovereignty, or *flaith*. Some Irish scholars have translated this word in a double sense, although there is disagreement on the matter. According to this interpretation *flaith* translates as "sovereignty" but also has associations in myth with strong drink or intoxication. Thus, we must conclude that the power of sovereignty granted to a king is itself intoxicating or is intoxication itself, and that it is gained through a drink. The source of this drink is the sacred spring that is identified with the goddess who is sovereignty herself. The myth of Niall and his four half brothers illustrates these symbolic identities clearly.

In this myth Niall and his brothers are given weapons by a smith,[14] and they go hunting in a wood. There they get lost and rest, building a fire to cook the game they have taken. One of the brothers, Fergus, is sent for water. He comes to a spring that is guarded by a black hag who demands a kiss in return for the water. Fergus refuses. The four other brothers follow, all refusing except Fiachra, who barely grazes her cheek. When Niall comes, he does not refuse but closes his eyes and kisses the hag. When he opens his eyes after the embrace, he beholds "the most beautiful woman in the world." This woman reveals herself as sovereignty (*Flaith*), gives him the drink, and states that he will be king and that his descendants will succeed him. The water from the well is likened to ale; that is, it is intoxicating: "Smooth shall be thy draught from the royal horn, 'twill be mead, 'twill be honey, 'twill be strong ale."[15]

Growing out of the multiple themes of intoxication as wisdom and sovereignty is that of erotic love leading to fecundity and regeneration. Eros in the well myths is symbolized by a woman. In the myth of Niall, she was in the form of a hag who was transformed into a beautiful maiden. In other texts, like *The Phantom's Frenzy* and *The Adventure of Nera*, she appears as a young woman and the intended bride of the male adventurer. Insofar as she is either presiding over or guarding the well, she must be understood as symbolically identical with it. Yet she is the bride who can never be brought into the ordinary world, for she dwells in the Otherworld. She is the ephemeral spirit of wisdom, sovereignty, and intoxication that can never be known but only intuited. She is the lover who can never be possessed.

The Adventure of Nera tells of a young man who on Samain Eve (October 31) entered the Otherworld through a cave located at the royal site of Connaught, Cruachan.[16] The Lord of the Otherworld directed him to the house of a young unmarried woman that was by the well before the fort in which the king lived. Each day Nera observed a blind man carrying a lame man to the well. Once they reached the well, the blind man would ask, "Is it there?" This event was mysterious to Nera, who asked the young woman, now his wife, what it meant. She told him that the king's golden crown was in the well. This image is symbolic of the union of the young man with sovereignty, wisdom, and eros. And indeed, later in the tale the young woman conceives and bears Nera a son, the future king, half god and half man.

It is myth, then, that is able through its context and language to give us some intuition of the ephemeral power present in the Irish sacred spring, a power that, like water, is elusive and transparent. Sometimes, like the guardian of the well, one can see this female power or presence, and at other times one sees through her, missing the subtlety of her form. First and foremost, myths speak of the well as a lady, a feminine form. She is the quintessence of wisdom, a wisdom that is intoxicating and erotic. It is this wisdom that enables life to be regenerated, this erotic power of water held by the earth as in a cup. He who drinks in this wisdom is sovereign and is able to husband the land, the lady. Thus the one given the wisdom by the lady is her husband but also her lover and her son. She is the earth, the place, the land at whose sacred center is the well, the source.

Ritual at the Celtic Springs

This descriptive understanding of the Irish sacred spring, granted us by myth, leads directly into the somatic dimension of the wells: the rituals that were used to enact this understanding physically and to make it efficacious. It is the ritual dimension of religion that brings into material form the un-manifest meanings of myth. But yet we must look again to myth to find the model for the ritual life that accompanies the mythic meaning of the wells. What we are interested in locating is a myth or myth complex that provides us with some ritual action that went on at or near formations of water. If our understanding of the well as a feminine erotic form is accurate, then we might find ritual models that involve some sexual union between a god or chieftain and a water goddess as a means of regenerating the earth and, perhaps, re-newing the authority and wisdom of the chief or god.

We find such activities in a series of myths in which the Dagda, perhaps the most ancient and most powerful of the Irish Celtic gods, is the primary male actor. The Dagda is a god who is remarkably different from the precon-ceived ideas we harbor of pagan deities, perhaps because these ideas are de-rived primarily from the dashing mythic pictures of the Greek gods painted for us by drama, poetry, and sculpture. The Dagda does not cut a fine figure of slim muscularity but rather is grotesque and even hideous in form. He is ugly. He is quite fat and has a huge potbelly. He wears a cowl and a short tunic, ordinarily the garments of a churl. His boots are of horsehide with the hair outside. He carries an enormous mallet or club, so large it is on wheels, and he is the possessor of a magical cauldron that constantly is filled with food and from which no one goes away unsatisfied. He is decidedly a figure associated with the earth and plays the role of companion to the mother god-dess. We shall see that he is also her lover.

His name translated means "the good god"—not good in the sense of kindness and purity but good in the sense of prowess and excellence. Further, the title implies that he is good at many things, not a specialist such as we see among the Greek gods. This notion of being good at many things is a model set for the Celtic gods in general by the Dagda and is termed in Irish *samildá-nach*, or man of many arts. This term, although used specifically in myth in reference to Lug, applies generally to all Celtic gods in varying degrees. Marie-Louise Sjoestedt in *Gods and Heroes of the Celts* emphasizes both the multiple functions of the gods as well as the fact that the Dagda was known for his many abilities.[17]

The Dagda is also named Eochaid Ollathair, which means All Father. Because genealogies of the gods tell us that the Dagda is not father of the gods, the name must imply a fathering role toward both gods and people. In other words, the Dagda is the archetypal paternal chieftain.[18]

Ruad Rófhessa is another of his names, which translates as Lord of Perfect Knowledge. Here we see one of the Dagda's primary features, his wisdom, which takes the form of magic when practiced. When we take into consideration the meanings of his names as well as the symbolism of his emblems, the Dagda presents himself as a god whose ambivalence focuses upon his solar ability to make war (symbolized by his club), his prodigious power of fecundation (symbolized by his cauldron and his slovenly appearance), and his omniscient wisdom in the form of magic. This paradox or ambivalence must be understood to be grounded in and made possible by the earth, that is, by the goddess. This fact is clearly symbolized by the wheels on the enormous club. In other words, the solar war-making ability "rides on" the earth, is made possible and is colored by the feminine. This notion also lends meaning to his ungainly appearance, which is cluttered and chaotic rather than smooth and open like the male solar divinities. His wisdom is magical, intuitive, and not analytic and calculating. Yet it is not the magic of the Hindu god Varuna, who uses nets to bind his foes, but the magic of vessels and cauldrons, of circles rather than lines. Thus, it distinguishes itself as a feminine wisdom possessed by the archetypal husband of the "place" and gained by union with her.

It follows that the moment of union between the All Father and the Earth Goddess is the moment of the making of a chief as well as the renewal of the goddess, the earth. What we are suggesting is that this union is the model for the inauguration ritual of chieftains that occurred at the center of the world with the guardian of the spring, the lady we have previously described. In our opinion the myth that serves as a model for this ritual is a myth concerning the Dagda and the Morrígan, the Irish goddess of death. In the myth the Dagda has a meeting with the Morrígan at the river Unius in Connaught. The meeting takes place on the eve of Samain, the Celtic new year that occurs on November 1. He finds the Morrígan straddling the river and bathing, her hair braided into nine loose tresses. The two make love, and afterward the

Morrígan warns the Dagda of the plans of his enemies and grants him her help.[19]

Although the event takes place at a river rather than a spring, the function of the source played by the spring is here played by the Morrígan herself. The straddling of the river symbolizes the waters of life flowing from her vagina, thus presenting her as the source, or the spring, as well as the mother goddess. Her nine tresses identify her as the supreme form of the Celtic triple goddess, the triple triangle, and may correspond to the nine hazel trees of Segais. Thus she is possessor of the complete wisdom of the goddess, that of the virgin, the mother, and the crone. This same symbolism of the source or spring of sacred waters of life is played by other goddesses, such as Medb in the *Táin Bó Cuailnge*. Here, at the end of the last battle between Connaught and Ulster, Medb, queen of Connaught (but also symbolic of the Great Goddess and Ireland), goes to a secret place to relieve herself. Her time of menstruation had arrived. "So Fergus [Medb's champion] took over the shelter of shields at the rear of the men of Ireland, and Medb relieved herself. It dug three great channels, each big enough to take a household."[20] It is said that these three channels are the sources of three sacred rivers of Ireland.

There are several other myths in which the symbolic identity of well-goddess-draft-cup-sovereignty is established. Two of them involve the hag at the well who is both the grantor of sovereignty to the prospective king and sovereignty herself. These are *Niall and the Hag at the Well*, about Niall and his four half brothers, and *Daire Doimthech's Five Sons*. In both of these tales the hag is embraced at the well and is transformed into a beautiful maiden, i.e., the renewed earth in springtime. The third, *Baile in Scail*, depicts the Lady of the Otherworld, Lady Sovereignty, giving a cup of *flaith derg*, or red truth/liquor, to Conn and predicting his kingship. The combined intentionality of these myths identifies the well with the sovereignty needed by the king and his drinking from it as both mating with the well/goddess and attaining sovereignty. T. F. O'Rahilly supports this notion in a comment on *Baile in Scail* when he says, "It is likely that in pagan times the acceptance by the bridegroom of a draught of liquor handed to him by the bride signified mutual consent to the marriage."[21]

In all of these instances, the goddess herself plays the role of the spring from which the creative force of regeneration comes. In the myth with the Dagda, this force is set into motion by the sexual union of the god and goddess at the time of the year's end. This, we suggest, is the mythic paradigm for the central rite that took place at the sacred springs of Celtic Ireland, the ritual of inauguration and the new year. In this ritual the chieftain-to-be mated with the land whose center or vagina was symbolized by the spring. This was accomplished in several ways, one including the actual lovemaking of the chieftain and a woman of sacral character symbolizing the "place," another by the drinking of water from the sacred spring, thus uniting with the fertilizing fluids of the goddess. Although evidence is scanty and incomplete, we can surmise that there were several other elements in the inauguration rite. One was the use of a sacred stone as a bed, or throne, upon which a chieftain was inaugurated.[22] It is also said that the stone screams at this time, thus confirming the correct choice of kings. We have already alluded to the *Lia Fáil,* originally located in the Otherworld, which performs this function. Another element was a sacred tree often located by the well. This tree was known as a *bile* in Irish, and it imitated the archetype of the nine hazel trees that stood by the Well of Segais in the Otherworld. It symbolized a source of wisdom, rooted in the past of the ancestors and linked to the sphere of the gods. In particular, the hazel tree is a magical tree associated with feminine wisdom through its bending to water. That is, hazel wood is used as a dowsing rod. It is also the tree from which the handle of the witch's broomstick is made.[23] In addition, at the inauguration, the king is given a straight white hazel wand as a symbol of his authority, a symbol of his possession of the wisdom of the goddess.[24]

Finally, we surmise that the king made a circuit around the well "sunwise," with his left shoulder toward the sea. This inference is based upon a variety of sources that, when viewed phenomenologically, attest to a pattern that lies at the foundation of the inauguration rite.

One of the most compelling sources regarding this circuiting is a tenth-century poem written by Cormacán Éigeas. It is an account of the circuit of all Ireland made by "Muircheartach, son of valiant Niall" upon his inauguration into the kingship of Tara.[25] From the text of the poem we see that the movement of the circuit is easterly from its starting point in Grianán Aileach, which is located in northwest Ulster. From the "fair province of Conchobhar" in southeast Ulster, Muircheartach moves into Leinster, on to Munster, thence to Connaught, and finally ends at Tara in Meath. Thus the direction of the circuit is clockwise, or sunwise, and always with the sea on the left.

To be sure, this text dates from the tenth century, long after the coming of Christianity, but R. A. S. Macalister suggests that the practice of circuiting by newly inaugurated kings is a very old one. It is said to have begun with Cormac in the third century on an Ireland-wide scale. Before that, according to Macalister, the high king, lacking extensive power over the entire island, presumably circuited only Tara itself.[26] The components of Tara are exactly the constituents of the holy well complex and include the sacred spring, tree, stone, and mound. It seems reasonable to infer from this that chieftains of the *tuaths* after their inauguration also circled the sacred spring complex, their center, with the "sea on their left." Finally, we see a continuity of this ritual circuiting at the holy wells today in the form of the round or pattern, in which pilgrims at the well walk around it, always sunwise, as a central part of their devotion.

This practice of kings circling their center sunwise is common cross-culturally within the history of religions. It amounts to the ritual of circumambulation. The idea of this symbolic ritual is that through the power of proximity and relationship, the one who circumambulates takes in the power of that which is circumambulated, and vice versa. Thus, the ritual establishes a kind of marriage between the king and the center, exactly what transpires in the Irish king's inauguration. We find the same practice among ancient Indian Buddhist kings. For example, King Mahasudanassa, after his inauguration, made a circuit around his entire dominion in the direction of the sun. This same ritual was performed by the ancient kings of Cambodia, and Macalister also mentions it taking place in Fiji.[27]

This last ritual action gives us insight into the symbolic identity of the living king. We suggest that he is identified with the sun in the sky, whereas his father or grandfather, whom he is destined to supplant as present husband to the goddess, is identified with the sun under the earth. The sun under the earth, or "black" sun, is master of the divine forge in which he crafts the magical weapons used by the "white" sun to bring about his demise.[28] The connection between the sun in the sky and the king is established by his consciously intended circuit sunwise. He imitates the sun and, by doing so in a ritual manner, symbolically identifies with it.

O'Rahilly makes clear the symbolic identity of the Otherworld lord with the sun and the connection of thunder and lightning with the sun. In talking about the *gai bulga*, or lightning weapon, he says, "The Sun-God, I may remark, was not only god of lightning and thunder; he was also lord of the

Otherworld." The Otherworld lord was the old god, the sun beneath the earth. In the sun's form as lightning, however, we see the younger god, what we have termed the "white sun," and it is this form of the sun god that was identified symbolically with the newly inaugurated king. O'Rahilly continues, "The lightning-weapon, I may explain, had its origin in the Otherworld, where it was forged by the Otherworld-god, the divine smith; but in myth we generally find it wielded by a younger and more human-like deity, the hero, as we may call him."[29]

Let us take a moment to summarize. By walking around the spring, the newly inaugurated king unites with the energy of the goddess present in the spring, thus symbolically mating with her, and at the same time, in the form of the young sun god, establishes the existence and boundaries of his realm, his spouse.

Let us look a bit more closely now at the sexual symbolism of the inauguration rite at the sacred spring. Evidence for this element of the ritual must be gleaned from various sources, for we have no extant text recording completely the inauguration ritual in Celtic times. We do know, however, that the name of the inauguration ritual was *banais righi,* which translates as a wedding feast of kingship. Thus the entire affair was conceived of as a marriage. The fact that the marriage implied a sexual union is evidenced by two things. First, the kingmaking at Tara was termed *feis temhra.* The word *feis* has a double meaning, as pointed out by Proinsias Mac Cana, and translates both as feast and as a night spent sexually with someone. Second, contained in the lore that surrounds Queen Medb are the many tales of her sexual exploits and a statement implying that whoever is to be king of Ireland must first sleep with her. "Truly great was the force and power of this Medb over the men of Ireland, for she it was who would not permit a king in Tara, unless he had her for his wife."[30]

As for other elements in the inauguration that we have suggested—the stone, the *bile,* and the wand—all are mentioned by P. W. Joyce in his description of the inauguration of post-Christian chieftains.[31] Finally, our general interpretation is confirmed by Mac Cana when he states: "The wedding ritual of *banais righi* evidently comprised two main elements, a libation, offered by the bride to her partner, and the coition."[32] The libation we take to be the drink from the well given by the lady of the well, his bride, which conveys *na bolcca immais* (bubbles of mystic inspiration) and symbolizes simultaneously his mating with her and his attainment of sovereignty.

Finally, we draw upon our fieldwork to support the mythological material indicating the central role of the sacred spring in the inauguration of kings. In an expedition to Ireland sponsored by Earthwatch in 1981, we made a survey of the major surviving inauguration sites of Celtic Ireland. At or near every inauguration complex we located a spring, usually now in use by Catholic Christians. One of the most striking instances of the well in association with the tree, stone, and mound was the O'Donnell inauguration site in Kilmacrennan, County Donegal. The site included a large rock mound and at its foot the well, Tobar an Duin, known locally as Doon Well (30). Our conjecture that this and other wells were used in the inauguration rite is supported by Ronald Hutton in his book *The Pagan Religions of the Ancient British Isles* when he writes, "The former [referring to the O'Donnell site] . . . is a rock with the famous holy well Tobar an Duin at its foot. It was presumably in this well that the king bathed."[33]

The king or chieftain, then, was married to the goddess of the place, his *tuath*, through ritual acts at the well. This "place" was defined by its natural configurations, through which its power emanated. Because the chieftain was married to this actual place, it was not possible to take land from others through warring activities. Rather, he could take hostages in the form of powerful persons; but the marriage of chief to place is never broken, and its center remained the sacred spring, site of the inauguration ritual.

Each place, or *tuath*, because of the varying topography of Ireland, had a different form of power. This difference in placehood was the basis for differences between families who dwelled in various *tuaths*, and it defined the clans that abided in each place. In our examination of hundreds of holy wells throughout Ireland, we discovered that there are three basic places, or contexts, in which the wells reside. These three differing contexts form three major types of *tuaths* within which are innumerable variations.

First, the great majority of wells are found at the center of some bowllike formation, and as such they form the source of that place. We call these wells umbilicus, or navel, wells. These are places of soft and fecundating power, much like that of a mother in her nurturing capacity. These are the most numerous of the three configurations and are nearly always found in a meadow or a boggy area.

St. Colman's Well near the town of Gort in County Galway (31) comes to mind as a fine example of the navel well. It is located in the center of a low-lying field and is immediately noticed because of the ornate cement canopy that covers the well. A sacred stone with an indentation that holds its power is just outside the door to the well, and by the stone is a large *bile,* or sacred tree, an ash that looms over the top of the well canopy.

The second form is less prevalent and is found in rocky or mountainous areas, often on mountain passes. Here the sense of power is hard and cutting, without flexibility, and yet the water is always exceptionally clean and pure, which may not be the case in the umbilicus wells. Sometimes these wells emerge from a cleft in the rock itself. In other cases the water is found in a hole in the rock that goes many feet into the earth. Often these wells are associated with the cure of the bones or teeth.

We found a wonderful example of a cleft well on the Burren, the "warm stone area" that is the high ridge dividing the central plateau in County Clare from the narrow ridge of field and beach hugging the sea. This is one of the wells that a local farmer, Paddy Nolan, told us about, explaining that it was a very ancient well and was good for the cure of sore teeth. This prehistoric well has only one name, the "Tooth Well," and no consecration to a saint, local or otherwise. The well, when we finally found it, was no more than six inches in diameter, a round hole in the solid limestone of the Burren that penetrated deeply into the core of the earth. There was a small, low stone niche or altar upon which were numerous sanctions, including bone fragments and teeth. The only evidence of Christian piety was a small wooden cross leaned against the back of the niche. Surrounding the well were two concentric stone circles, evidence of its ancient Celtic heritage.

The third context, the most interesting to us, was found by the sea, sometimes a few yards inland, sometimes at the very edge of the shore, or, less often, within the tidal surf, being covered over most of the time. These wells are rich in symbolism, the most obvious of which is the periodic union between the salt and fresh water, the Great God and Goddess. Here fecundity was of paramount importance, and often we would find "serpent eggs" beside the well, placed there by women who hoped to become pregnant.

An outstanding example of a sea well is found near the town of Ballyshannon in County Donegal. The well is dedicated to St. Patrick (32) and is located on a beach on the shore of the river Erne just before it pours into Donegal Bay. The well itself is keyhole shaped and, again, reminds one of a vagina. Its flow of water is full and clear and spills across the beach at low tide into the river Erne, which is very wide at this point. Close by the well is

St. Patrick's Well, Ballyshannon, Co. Donegal (32). Seawater
fecundates this freshwater well at highest moon tides.

St. Patrick's Well, Ballyshannon, Co. Donegal (32). A sea
well with iron crosses denoting each ritual station.

a small thorn bush that is covered with clooties. Surrounding the well in a huge circle is a series of fourteen white metal crosses that form the stations of the cross, which are a part of the pattern at the well. At high tide the seawater rushing up the river Erne rises up the beach, covering the well with its fertilizing waters.

The feeling of power at these sea wells was one of youth and freshness, and sometimes of awe and fear at the approach of the tide and its inevitable covering over of the well. At one location, St. Caillin's near Ballyconneely in County Galway (33), we found by the well a spiral pattern set out with serpent eggs. The pattern was used as a kind of labyrinth and was part of the ritual at the well. Here again the spiral is associated both with the sea and with the cyclical nature of fertility.

These three contexts are symbolically important in several ways. The Rees brothers speak of the Three Wells of the Ocean, found in Welsh myth, which parallel exactly the three contexts we observed in Ireland. The first is the sea flood. The second, the fall of rain through the atmosphere. The third "comes through the veins of the mountains like the flinty feast made by the King of Kings." [34] Here the three contexts symbolize the three spheres of the cosmos: the sky (mountains), the atmosphere (rain), and the earth (sea flood).

Although the ritual marriage at the well was one of regeneration, it was frequently held on the festival of Samain, the new year festival, which is a time open to death. At this time the boundaries between the Otherworld and this world are loosened, making movement possible back and forth. In addition, sacrificial death took place as part of the festival. In effect, through the mating of the chieftain to the place, he was sacrificed to the goddess through his loss of self in various forms. Implementing the loss was the intoxication that was a form of the power of wisdom passed on to the king through this marriage. In his intoxication, both literal and symbolic, the king loses himself, is dead to the ordinary, and passes into the realm of the Otherworld. Further, he loses his life, freely giving it through his semen in the mating ritual. It is thought by many scholars that actual regicide took place as the virility of the king waned. [35]

The king, then, is offered or sacrificed to the goddess in her various forms. Through this sacrifice and death, new life is possible, just as through the death of the seed, the new plant arises. The well also functions as the goddess. Skulls and bones have been discovered in the wells. [36] Here the well is goddess in her form as hag, the receptacle of death through whose flood of blood the earth and the king are regenerated.[37]

Ritual offerings to the well as goddess are not limited to the kingship ceremony, however. Several large finds of votive deposits have been uncovered that indicate ritual use of wells and other bodies of water. Even today one finds that pilgrims to the holy wells have a strong urge to throw some personal article into the well. Most often one finds money in the wells, while numerous other objects are left around the wells, such as religious statues, pins, prayers, bits of clothing, pictures, pens, and rosaries. The archetype of transformation and regeneration through death and sacrifice remains with us today, but in a disguised and infantilized form. Regeneration through sacrifice and death has degenerated into the fulfillment of wishes by means of the offering of money to the well. Thus the common folk motif of the wishing well.

As we stand back and think at a distance upon the symbolism of the sacred spring, its myths and rituals, the role of the well in Celtic Ireland emerges as crucial to life, both physical and spiritual. It is no wonder that its use has persisted from the Celtic tradition into Christianity and beyond that into an infantilized secular form. For it is the well that is the source of wisdom, a wisdom of the earth little known in modern times yet still lurking beneath the surface of the spring. It is a wisdom that, like water itself, holds all the possibilities of life, from knowledge of the nature of things to the urge to regenerate through sacrifice and love. The hazel trees still drop their berries into the clear water of the spring to be eaten by the salmon of knowledge. We have only to gaze beneath the surface to see the fish.

3

Loric Power at the Wells

Loric and Sacred Space

IN STUDYING THE sacred springs of Ireland, we have stressed the observation that the ancient Irish religion was based upon the sacrality of the earth. Ireland, the place, was considered to be divine and took the image of a goddess such as Medb or Brigid or the Morrígan. She was the Great Mother, the giver of all life and the bringer of death. She was the earth who regenerated herself through her mating with the lord of the place, or *tuath*, who was then granted the wisdom and power to order the world. He became her husband and in doing so was married to the land. We call such earth-centered religions cosmic, in line with Eliade's use of the term.

The emphasis in cosmic religions is upon the power of space rather than the power of time, as is found in historical religions. There is a further refinement in the emphasis upon space that is found in Celtic Irish religion. Before the tenth century A.D. there was no high king who ruled over the entire island. Rather, there were many small chieftains, each married to a small piece of land that he held in common with various kin who made up a clan. Consequently, there was no notion of the concept of world in a universal sense. Instead, Ireland was constituted by a mosaic of "places" in the manner in which we have used the term heretofore.

The power of place contrasts with the power of world. The overall sense one gets from the essence of world, or what we choose to call worldhood, and the sacred is that of expansion and universality. That is, power moves out from a center to the boundaries of the world, and beyond if possible. An apt image for this form of power is that of a wagon wheel whose hub is the center and whose spokes carry power from there to the rim, which functions as a boundary. Within the boundary of the world a common order exists to which everyone assents. For example, in ancient Egypt during the period of empire, there was a single monarch whose power was in command throughout the entire Egyptian "world." At one point there was even introduced a single or universal god who was to reign over all Egypt. Worldhood and the sacred, then, incorporate universal forms or models that apply to all people. They constitute a power that is generated through the exact repetition of myths and rituals in the same way throughout the world.

There is another form of power, however, that is place maintaining rather than world creating. Where this form of power is predominant we find a series of characteristics that are at opposite poles to those of the sacred. The overall sense one gets from the power generated by the essence of a place or placehood is that of implosiveness and particularity. Power seems to fold in on itself, from center to boundaries and back again to center. One gets a feeling of coziness and containment, a feeling of being present or grounded in just a certain way. Within the place power arises from the differences among its inhabitants and the configurations of the landscape. The basis of this power, then, is otherness rather than sameness, particularity rather than universality. We choose to call this form of power the loric, in that it is the lore of a thing or place that fills it with the fascination we hold for things homemade and thus not perfect, things cozy and thus confining, in short, things "other" and thus different from ourselves. To be sure, the sacred contains otherness and the loric contains universality, but the predominant force in each form seems to overshadow its opposite rather than bring it into balance.[1]

Celtic Ireland was constituted by a patchwork of places in which there was little sense of world and in which the power of the loric predominated. Even after the coming of Christianity and the establishment of the high king at Tara or Emain Macha, the power of the loric was retained within the small *tuaths*,[2] and the chieftains remained married to the place, their life source, and the place existed parallel to the newly emerging world of Ireland. It might even be said that the advent of worldhood in Ireland might never have occurred had it not been for the coming of Christianity with its universalizing and catholic tendencies.

The *tuath*, then, continued to exist after the high king was created because of the power of its placehood, which is essentially the power of a certain form of space. Here we are dealing with loric, not sacred, space. Loric space is space that is for the most part unique: there is nothing like it anywhere else. Loric space beckons and then contains one in its aura of power. One is happy there, satisfied just to be where one is and to live out one's life at the source. This source within Irish culture was, and still remains to a certain extent, the holy well. Thus the holy well is the source of loric power, which emanates outward and then back upon itself, drawing all within its purview to drink from its waters.

There is a place called Kerry Head jutting out into the Atlantic Ocean in County Kerry. Here dwells the family clan of the Corridans, who occupy the greater part of the head. The family dwellings are clustered about the ruins of an old church and burial ground dedicated to St. Erc, an Irish saint of the area. Located within the burial ground is a standing stone, clearly of prehistoric origin, upon which rests an egg stone. Michael Corridan, titular head of the Corridans, told us that the egg stone never leaves or falls from its perch atop the menhir. Once, many years ago, a malcontent stole the stone, put it on his cart, and started up the hill from the graveyard. The horse could not pull the cart up the hill, and the stone rolled out and assumed its place once again atop the standing stone. The world must go on re-creating itself; the egg stone must remain atop the menhir.

Of still greater interest is a well that is located between the church site and the sea. Between the well and the church site stands Michael Corridan's house. When we talked with Michael in 1980, he showed us a stone that he kept in a paper bag atop his mantel in the kitchen. This stone, according to Michael, remains always cool and moist, even on the driest and warmest days of summer. But what was of even greater interest was that when the stone was placed in the well, the power of the well was activated, and this could be done only by a blood Corridan. No one who married into the family could use the stone effectively. Still further, the healing power of the well worked only on blood Corridans.

In these still-living traditions of the Corridans of Kerry Head, we see the power of the loric manifested on several levels and in various ways. To begin with, the Corridan compound manifests the implosive power of loric space. It is differentiated by its geographical uniqueness and by the total and absolute identification of the family with the place. The power of the place, however, does not extend beyond the perimeter of Kerry Head. Nor can anyone enter the place and participate in that power, which is limited to that land and the people who originated there.

The Corridan compound on Kerry Head is a self-contained and self-regenerating place with no dependence upon the external world, spiritually or physically. It gives birth to, sustains, heals, and buries its own. The holy well plays the role of center and place of orientation. In addition, it is the source of life and regeneration through its healing power. Because the power of the well is limited to the Corridans born on the head, the nature of that power is loric, not sacred. To be sure, the healing force of the well is understood as being supernatural and numinous, a quality it has in common with the sacred, but the numinosity manifests itself as intimacy and cannot be approached by those not born from the "place." The well carries with it an awesome power that does not extend beyond the head. Once on the head, the outsider enters an "other world" that, because of the power of intimacy, is fearful and strange.

The focus of Kerry Head is upon the particularity of the geographical surroundings that situate the well and the people who dwell there and upon the particular nature of the water of the well itself, that is, its particular healing power. Each *tuath* in ancient Ireland, and indeed each well, had a *deus loci*, or deity of the place, whose spirit was the power that permeated the area and dwelled in the spring. On Kerry Head it was St. Erc. This spirit was unique, did not point beyond itself, and may not have been known a few valleys away. Thus Ireland did not have a fixed and universal pantheon such as one finds in Greece. There were few deities that were known and worshiped throughout the island, and even they were associated with some place and were not abstract celestial or universal sovereigns. The holy well, then, was a paradigm of loric space, infused with the spirit of the place, usually a goddess, to whom the tribe owed allegiance and from whom they were born. Because of their ontological connection with the place, the clan chief was thought of as related to the *deus loci*. Thus, even today importance of patrimony and place of origin in Ireland remains vital, and modern Irishmen, both on and off the island, maintain an inordinate interest in genealogy. This interest must be understood as evidence of the continuing influence of loric power as manifest in space.

Loric Themes at the Wells

Some of the most interesting results of our research and fieldwork were the identification of a series of loric themes that attach themselves to the wells. These themes are constituted by particular objects of power or tale motifs that are associated with a particular well or that are found at many wells. It is more often the case that the theme is found at several wells. Despite the apparent universality of several themes, we must understand the power contained within them as loric rather than sacred. This is the case because of their connection with the place and because they have no relationship to a universal or world-creating mythos. Thus the fact that a supernatural tree may appear at many wells is not known by the people associated with the various wells, nor is it a concern to them. It is not necessary to have a special tree at the well in the sense that it is necessary to have a crucifix in every sanctuary within a Catholic church. The presence of the crucifix is a universal and world-creating phenomenon known and accepted by all the members of the "body of Christ," whereas the appearance of the tree is only of local or loric concern.

The venerated tree is one of the themes found at holy wells, but it may not appear at all wells; this is its loric nature. There is no doubt about the fact that at the most fundamental level, the tree at the well participates in the symbolism of the tree of life. The Irish Celtic context of the tree, however, can provide us with some further amplifications of this symbol from the perspective of loric power. One of these amplifications is the association of the hazel tree, by means of its nuts (or berries) falling into the Well of Segais, with wisdom and sovereignty. This association is based upon the Celtic reverence for the human head, which itself was a source of power.[3] The hazel nut, or any nut, through visual and structural resemblance symbolizes the head, while the meat of the nut symbolizes the brain.[4] Thus to eat the nut is to gain wisdom.

The hazel tree is one of the trees of the Celtic tree calendar. Its time of the year is from August 5 to September 1, and it is the ninth tree on the calendar. The hazel is one of the witching trees or trees of divination. This is because of its attraction to water, the source of intuitive wisdom gained through divination. The hazel wand bends to water and is therefore used by dowsers.[5]

Despite the connection of the hazel tree with the archetypal Well of Segais in the Otherworld, the hazel tree is rarely found in association with holy wells of this world. In our fieldwork we found that the most prevalent tree by far was the thorn tree, especially the whitethorn, or hawthorn. This observation is corroborated by A. T. Lucas in his article "The Sacred Trees of Ireland," in which he surveyed the presence of sacred trees at 210 holy wells throughout Ireland. In this sampling he found that 103 of these trees were thorn or whitethorn, 75 were ash, 7 were oak, 6 willow, 5 elder, 4 holly, 3 rowan, 3 alder, 2 elm, 1 yew, and 1 fir.[6]

Although the predominance of the whitethorn at holy wells today does not amplify the archetypal myth of the well, this tree nonetheless possesses a notable symbolism appropriate to the present-day functions of the wells. The thorn tree is a spirit tree, again one of the trees of the ancient Celtic tree calendar, its place on the calendar being May 13–June 9.[7] Perhaps the major reason the thorn tree is associated with the spirit is because of its ability to penetrate from outer to inner worlds. In other words, it breaks the skin and allows entry of the healing spirit through the open wound. For this reason the thorn is associated with inner healing, or a healing of the soul. The practice at holy wells today of placing or tying pieces of clothing, called clooties, about the limbs of the venerated tree places an emblem of the person in constant contact with the penetrating power of the thorn and thus provides a perpetual source of inner healing. In addition, the thorn tree, because of its ability to injure, becomes a protective barrier to the desecration of the well.

But there is a positive aspect to this function of protection. The act of passing through the thorn trees in order to obtain the wisdom-giving water of the well is an initiatory act that purifies the initiate through the sacrifice of blood on the tree. We find the same initiatory function in the tale of the sleeping princess, asleep in her castle surrounded by thorns. The hero prince must cut his way through the thorny barrier and there kiss the princess awake. His effectiveness in this action is assured by the initiatory death brought about in his struggle and spilling of blood on the thorns.[8]

Clooties are still found on venerated trees around the holy wells all over Ireland. We found outstanding examples at Lady Well near the village of Abbey in County Galway (34) and at Doon Well near Kilmacrennan, County Donegal. These two wells are particularly interesting because of their ancient

Lady Well, Abbey, Co. Galway (34). A fine example of a "rag tree."

origins. These early origins are indicated at Lady Well by the series of small mounds within the enclosure of the well complex. These mounds are considered sacred by the Christians now using the well, and they are circumambulated as part of the pattern ritual. The mounds themselves have nothing whatsoever to do with Christian symbolism, but they do retain the Celtic symbolism of the mound, or *síd,* swelling with the power of the goddess. At a later date they were considered to be inhabited by fairies.

Doon Well presents us with clear Celtic features, the most prominent of which is Doon Hill, or Doon Rock. The hill is a steep outcropping about fifty yards from the well. It was on this hill that the chieftains of Tír Chonaill, the O'Donnells, were inaugurated for many centuries. The last to be inaugurated on this spot was Niall Garbh O'Donnell in 1603.[9] Local folk also claim

Doon Well, Kilmacrennan, Co. Donegal (30). The rock is
the hill behind the well, inauguration site of the
O'Donnells.

Doon Well, Kilmacrennan, Co. Donegal (30). Clooties
that have touched the site of pain are tied on a bush to
effect a cure.

Doon Well, Kilmacrennan, Co. Donegal (30). A great
burden of clooties places the pain or disease upon a
tree or sacred bush.

that there is a cave within the hill, now hidden or covered over, indicating that the hill was at one time considered to be a *síd* or fairy mound. *Síds* were also perceived by the Irish Celts to be locations of the Otherworld.

The venerated tree by Doon Well is a remarkable one. To begin with, it is a hazel tree, so the complex is even more in keeping with the archetypal well, the Well of Sagais in the Otherworld. The hazel tree is small, only five and one-half feet tall, but it is completely covered with all manner of clooties so that it appears to be bending under the pain and sickness of all the world. Beside and in front of the tree are about sixty stakes pounded into the ground. These too are covered with clooties and other sanctions. Among the stakes is a twenty-six-inch statue of Christ also covered with clooties. To carry the clootie theme still further, there are two flat stones to the right of the hazel tree as one faces the well. The sacrality of these stones is marked by all types of sanctions and clooties that are either attached to or resting upon the stones. These include such things as gloves, handkerchiefs, T-shirts, stockings, scarves, sweaters, towels, pens, pencils, keys, pins, as well as rosaries, scapulars, prayer cards, and small statues of saints. These stones present us with a lucid example of the synthesis of Celtic and Christian traditions.

One other tree associated with a holy well is worth mentioning. This place is named Seir Kieran (35) and is located near Clareen in County Offaly. It is of particular interest because of its location in the middle of a main highway. The two lanes of the road were separated in order not to disturb the tree. The well itself is approximately one-fourth mile away in the center of a low-lying field. Once again, the tree is a whitethorn, and its power is still active as witnessed by the numerous clooties we saw attached to it. In addition, several rosaries as well as a holy picture were hanging on the tree. Coins had been placed in crevices in the tree and were also found lying beneath the tree. We last visited this well in 1980.

The most remarkable sacred tree encrusted with sanctions was found at St. Lassair's Well in County Roscommon. The well complex is located by the side of Lough Meelagh near the town of Ballyfarnan. This well also has Celtic evidence in the form of a table stone that is said to contain healing powers for the back. Tree worship, of course, predates Christian entry into Ireland, and this ancient tree in association with the table stone gives further credence to St. Lassair's early origin. The tree is a great ash, and as far up as a tall man can reach, it is almost entirely encrusted with coins, rosaries, pins,

holy medals, and other sanctions that are pushed into crevices in the bark. This practice has been going on for many years, for many of the coins and other objects have been nearly covered by the growth of the tree.

Another variant of the sanctions-embedded-in-tree motif is located at St. Fechin's Well and Abbey in Fore, County Westmeath (36). This one is particularly interesting because it is dead physically but still alive spiritually through the hundreds of coins that continue to be hammered into the trunk. There is only a fragment of the tree remaining, and it stands only about four or five feet tall. The monastery was founded there by St. Fechin in the seventh century, so the tree is of ancient vintage. It is said to be an ash, and our informant, Finian Bell, told us that the wood will not burn. He said that when his mother was a young woman, a man chopped off a branch of the tree for

St. Lassair's Well, Lough Meelagh, Co. Roscommon (15). Sacred tree showing implants of coins, rosaries, and nails.

firewood and the next day was found dead. Bell was about thirty years of age when we visited this well in 1987. There is another sacred ash, this one alive and well, about two hundred yards away by the side of St. Fechin's Bath. St. Fechin is said to have lain in this pool at night as part of a prayer vigil. It is also said that children were healed at this pool. Finally, we were informed that the ash is to St. Fechin what the shamrock is to St. Patrick.

In summing up our discussion of the venerated tree at the holy well, we want to emphasize the fact that reverence for living trees finds no place within Roman Catholicism. Continued reverence for trees and the attribution to them of healing or other power are based upon the Celtic worship of trees and the incorporation of sacred trees into a lunar calendar, which gave meaning through the tree symbolism to the cycle of the year. Further, trees were powerful symbols of the past and of the ancestors because of their longevity, their ability of self-renewal, and their rootedness in the Otherworld, the womb of the goddess. Because of these roots, they possessed the healing power of the goddess and provided access to the wisdom of the Otherworld. In other words, they functioned as inverted *axes mundi*. Finally, it is not mere coincidence that we find that the trees that are sacred to the Celtic calendar, such as the ash, hazel, and whitethorn, are the very trees that are still revered by Christians at the holy wells today.

Another of the major loric themes appearing at the holy well is that of the venerated stone. Once again, the presence of venerated or healing stones at holy wells in Ireland today is possible because of the Celtic mythological model. One of the waves of invaders that established Ireland in mythic time was the Tuatha Dé Danann. When they arrived in Ireland, according to some versions they came flying through the sky enshrouded in a dark mist.[10] They alighted upon Conmaicne Rein, and for three days thereafter the darkness of their mist hid the sun. These were the magicians and sorcerers of Ireland and were later to become fairies. They brought with them the four talismans or archetypes that were the source of mystical power both in the Otherworld and on the surface. One of these talismans was the *Lia Fáil*. It was this stone that was used in the inauguration ritual at the well and that screamed when the next intended king touched it. Because kingship was not hereditary in early times, it was an important determinant in choosing the right heir to the kingship. The *Lia Fáil*, then, was the mythical model for the various types of sacred stones that are found in a loric context at the holy wells today.

Let us look at some of the lore that now surrounds stones at holy wells and then attempt to arrive at a general symbolic understanding of the stone at the well and its roots in the mythic past. There are three types of stones at wells: stones as tables, stones as heads, and stones as beds or seats. Each of these configurations of stones appears frequently at wells, though the stone as a head seems to be the most prevalent.

To say that the stone at the well functions symbolically as a head is already an interpretation. It is, however, an interpretation that the prevailing evidence fully justifies. Anne Ross, in her extensive discussion of the Celtic cult of the head, suggests that "the cult of the head amongst the Celts manifests itself in yet another way, namely in its seemingly fundamental association with venerated waters." [11] When the head stone is in association with the well, it renders the well magical, that is, the stone activates the power of the well that gives forth wisdom, fecundity, and prophecy. Fertility is at the base of both wisdom and prophecy because of the fact that he who is fertile, she who is pregnant, knows the future and thus is full of the wisdom of prophecy.

Fertility is associated with the head in Celtic tradition because of its connection with foliage, grain, and wealth. Ross cites the blending of foliage with images of the human head in her study, and foliage is symbolic of a blooming land, a blooming goddess. Further evidence of fertility as associated with the head is present in the image of the head of a god vomiting money. [12] Money is gold, phenomenologically speaking, and is evidence of material wealth. It is evidence of fullness and ripeness, and, as gold, it is the sun within the earth, that is, the lord of the Otherworld and the husband/fecundator of the goddess. Finally, we find the head stone as a symbol of the head of grain that is the seed and the source of life for the people. In other words, the head of grain is the chieftain and husband of the waiting land. Often this head stone is mounted upon a pillar stone, which is interpreted by most scholars to be a phallus. Our suggestion that the head stone on the pillar symbolizes the stalk of grain does not rule out the phallic interpretation but places alongside it an equally compelling and perhaps more ecologically appropriate possibility, since we have already seen the head associated with plant life.

Some examples will serve to amplify our suggestions about the sacred stone at the well as head. There is a well-known sacred spring near Ardfert in County Kerry called Tobar na Molt, or "Well of the Wethers." What is of

Well of the Wethers (a St. Patrick's well), Ardfert, Co.
Kerry (10). Inside view of hostel for overnight pilgrims.

Well of the Wethers (a St. Patrick's well), Ardfert, Co.
Kerry (10). Altar showing the "saints'" heads that are
rubbed and ritually incised for healing.

particular interest to us in this context is the stone table, used as an altar, into which have been inlaid three heads of stone. It is clear that these heads are considered to be sacred as they are inscribed deeply over the face with the shape of a cross. Inscribing the heads thus is part of the pilgrimage to the well and enables the pilgrim to gain power from the stone.[13] The style of the heads is Celtic in design, and they appear to be very old, perhaps symbolic of earlier gods, though they are now said to represent saints Brendan, Collumcille, and Ita. Another ancient site is the well of St. Ciaran near the Abbey of Clonmacnoise, County Offaly (37), which he founded in A.D. 548–49. This well is probably also of Celtic origin because it is near the river Shannon, sacred to the Celts. By the well stands a venerated tree, a white-thorn without thorns, and at the head of the well in a semicircle stand three stone monuments of differing shapes but in our opinion all representing the head. Part of the round at this well is the kissing of these heads by the pilgrim.[14]

The most famous example of the head upon the pillar stone is located at St. Olan's Well in Aghbullogue, County Cork (38), and is known as St. Olan's Cap. This round stone, or head, sits upon an ogham-inscribed pillar, which again attests to its Celtic roots. Further, the touching of the stone is said to cure headaches. The other head-on-pillar is located in the Corridan compound on Kerry Head. This one is dedicated to St. Erc. Both stones have legends associated with them that tell of their being stolen from atop the pillar and then having returned by their own accord.

Two other forms of the head stone as fertilizing agent are of interest. The first are the egg-shaped stones, also headlike in form, that function as sanctions at various wells. One such well with these sanctions is St. Fechin's Well on Omey Island, Claddaghduff, County Galway. This well is a sea well, located on the shore of the island with a long stone-lined entrance from the well to the sea. The action of the tides at full moon fecundates the well through the vagina-shaped stone enclosure around the well. On the top of the enclosure are to be found several rounded or egg-shaped stones, which we were told were called "serpent eggs."[15] The stones are placed there as part of the round at the well by women hoping to become pregnant. Another well at which serpent eggs are found is St. Attracta's Well near Monasteraden, County Roscommon (39). Here the stones have been formalized in that several of them are cemented into the top of the stone enclosure that surrounds

St. Ciaran's Well, Clon-
macnoise, Co. Offaly
(37). One of the three
stone heads that are
kissed and marked during
rounds or "patrons."

St. Erc's Well, Listowel, Co. Kerry (23). Pre-Christian
standing stone in the Corridan compound with stone
"head" that cannot be moved.

St. Erc's Well, Listowel, Co. Kerry (23). Michael Corridan,
family patriarch (recently deceased), holding the
Booley stone that activates this well.

St. Fechin's Well, Omey Island, Co. Galway (26). This sea
well shows many egg stones that are thought to be dragon
or serpent eggs petrified by St. Patrick.

the well. There is one large freestanding egg stone at the center of this enclosure.

The second form of head stone as fertilizing agent has a bit more circuitous
path of fertility symbolism, but it is all the more interesting. Near St. Peakaun's Well in the Glen of Aherlow, County Tipperary, there stands the ruin
of his ancient church. Just outside the church wall is a large stone upon which
are found two smaller, obviously venerated stones. These stones are head-
shaped, and we were told by our informant, John Burke, who owns the land,
that one is a butter stone and the other a cursing stone. The butter stone is
of particular interest because of its fertilizing or life-giving powers. The stone
was placed in the butter churn as a magical aid to promote the formation of
the butter. In other words, the stone fertilized the mother milk, causing her

St. Peakaun's Well, Glen
of Aherlow, Co. Tipper-
ary (19). Butter stone and
cursing stones are found
in association with this
well.

to give birth to the butter child. Butter itself, as child of the goddess-cow-milk symbolic complex, was a potent fecundating agent and was associated with holy wells. It was often thrown into a well as a means of activating the healing power of the well, and then cows were driven through the well to restore them to health.[16] Thus, the butter stone may have been placed in the well (as churn or vessel) to activate its power. Such a practice took place at the Corridan well on Kerry Head, where the venerated stone, or Booley stone, was placed in the well to activate its healing powers. This stone was always cool and moist, like butter. In addition, in centuries past the year's supply of butter was made in the summer pasture high in the hills in a house known as the Booley House.[17] Thus, the Corridan Booley stone may well have been a butter stone. The butter stone, then, is the head of the son of the goddess-cow-milk, and as such is her son, lover, and husband in the ancient Celtic tradition.

Another major configuration of the sacred stone is that of the stone table. The most common form of such a table is that of a large flagstone supported by four pillar stones. The table has the look of a small dolmen and, we think, functions symbolically in the same way. The dolmen is usually a very large stone supported by other stones. It is frequently high enough for a person to pass under standing up, and it is thought to be the entrance to a grave site that has since been destroyed. Thus, the dolmen functions symbolically as a threshold, a point of passage from one world to the next, and a point, because of its stone composition, that is timeless and eternal. Passage through the dolmen is equivalent to transformation from one state of being to another.

It is interesting that, in two cases of table stones at wells, the top of the table is not the primary point of power. Rather, the power lies beneath the table, and the person seeking transformation is asked to pass beneath the stone. St. Lassair's Well, located by the shore of Lough Meelagh and between the villages of Ballyfarnan and Keadue in County Roscommon, not only has a remarkable ash tree but a stone table that consists of a large flag raised about two feet off the ground by four smaller stones. Upon this table rests a large egg stone, some blessed clay, and various other sanctions. We were informed that once a year the bishop says Mass upon this stone. But the primary power of the stone is derived from crawling under it to gain healing power for the back. Just as the power of mountains in the Celtic context lies not on top but within the mountain, so, too, the power of the table stone is beneath or within it. This same ritual of passing under the table is found in Ardmore, County Waterford, at St. Declan's Well (40). Near the well on the beach there lies St. Declan's stone, again a large flagstone, upon which St. Declan traveled to Ireland. On St. Declan's Day, July 24, this stone is part of a pilgrimage and is crawled under as a means of healing backaches. In both these cases not only is the power found within the table stone, but the stone continues to be associated with bones in the same way that cleft wells emerging from rock tend to provide cures for bone ailments, including teeth.

There are a few variations of the table theme worth mentioning. Often the sacred flagstone provides a tabletop over the well itself. We find a good example of this at Doon Well in County Donegal. Here the top of the table is strewn with all manner of sanctions, but the true source of the power resides beneath the table as the spring. At Tobernault near the city of Sligo, there is a Mass rock that is said to have been used as an altar during penal times, a period of severe Catholic persecution by the British during the seventeenth century. Clearly, however, the rock predates the eighteenth century as does the entire well complex. The stone is probably of pre-Christian origin and has a concave curvature on the top edge. Pilgrims rest their back into this curvature to obtain healing. Also on the top of this stone is a series of small concave indentations that are said to be the fingerprints of St. Patrick. Pilgrims place their fingertips within them to participate in the power of the saint that is retained there.

The final configuration of stone at the well is the bed or seat. The example of St. Patrick's fingerprints in the stone also shares in the intentionality or essence of the bed or seat. As before, it is the symbolism of interiority that is at play in the stone bed. In this case, the interiority takes the form of container or vessel within which one reposes as part of a ritual pattern at the well. The vessel is well known as a symbol of the goddess and the feminine in general.[18] It expresses the ambivalence of the womb as both that which contains and thus inhibits and that which nurtures, enabling growth. Thus, to be within the vessel is to be within the goddess and to be alternately contained and nurtured by her. The earth, of course, is the macrocosmic vessel and the Great Goddess herself. Mountains present us with an intermediary level of the symbol and the stone container or bed with yet a smaller correlate. The sacred spring also is a vessel, but one that both contains and releases, though the symbolism of release through the ever-emerging water is

65

predominant. In addition, the spring has a hole in the bottom, which is itself a threshold providing entrance into the body of the goddess and allowing her nurturing blood/milk/water to emerge in an endless and continual stream for the benefit of us, her children. The stone bed, then, is symbolic of the womb of the goddess, which heals, protects, and gives birth.

Essentially the stone bed is a container that holds one within its concave shape. It often functions as a seat in which transformation takes place. The clearest example of this that we found was at a place known as the Earl's Well near the town of Kildare in County Kildare (41). The central attraction of this site was not the well itself but a large stone known as the chair of Kildare. It was upon this stone that the earls of Kildare were inaugurated. Thus the stone was a seat within which the transformation from layman to sacred king, husband of the land, took place. It was the seat or source of his power, the crucible in which his rebirth took place. A similar stone sits at the coronation site of the earls of Thomond, Magh Adhair, near the town of Quin in County Clare (42). In the case of this stone, however, the function was not that of seat or throne but rather of basin or secondary well. The stone itself sits near the mound that marks the site of the coronation. It is a large stone, about two yards in circumference and about three feet high. On the top of the stone there is a depression approximately twelve by eighteen inches. This basin held water to be used by the prospective king to wash himself before the coronation. There was also, imbedded in the rock, a red stone that the initiate is said to have used as soap.[19]

A second example of the stone bed as basin is found on Devinish Island, County Fermanagh (43). This stone is called St. Molaisse's Bed and is a stone trough that is embedded in the ground near the saint's house. The stone is about six feet long and fifteen inches wide. It contains the power for the healing of backaches, and the afflicted party lies in the trough or bed and repeats a series of prayers.[20] A final example of the bed stone is found at St. Patrick's Well and Bed near Maumeen, County Galway (44), in the Maam Turk mountains. The fact that the bed is mentioned in the name of the well is evidence of its importance in the minds of the people. Here the bed is not a freestanding stone but is carved out of a cliff on the west side of the pass in which the well is located. It is clearly in association with the well and is across from and slightly above it in the hillside. There is no evidence as to how the bed is used. Also in association with this well are numerous other stone formations, all retaining some sacrality. There are four stone circles, three standing stones, and a stone pole in the shape of a pyramid. Of these formations, it is the stone circles that retain the function of the vessel that we observed in the stone beds. The circles appear to be intended to mark off a sacred area or area of power. This seems to be the case because the interiors of three of the circles are worn bare and that of the fourth circle is filled with small stones.

This intention of the stone circle is borne out at St. Caillin's Well, Ballyconneely, County Galway. Here are found, in addition to the well dedicated to St. Caillin, patron saint of sailors, two stone circles. One of these circles has within it a series of concentric circles in the shape of a spiral. Also found within this circle is an assortment of sanctions including buttons, coins, rosary beads, bits of glass, and pieces of religious statues. Obviously the interior of the circle, which has a diameter of about eight feet, is considered to be a place of power; that is, it is a container of power, a vessel. The second stone circle is much larger, being fifty-seven feet in diameter. Within it are found many small stones and the same assortment of sanctions as found in the other circle. Both circles thus function as containers of power in a similar fashion as the well itself. In common is the configuration of vessel or container of power into which are thrown or placed offerings intended to put the giver in direct contact with the power through the mediation of the object offered to the vessel. In addition, it appears possible that the pilgrims place themselves physically within the circle, for the concentric circles within the one complex may function as a labyrinth.

Stone, Tree, Water: The Holy Well Complex

The combination of stone, tree, and water taken together forms a primary symbolism. It points beyond itself to the cosmos and, through resemblance to that cosmos, participates in it. This is the primary function of symbols. The stone, tree, water complex presents us with a miniature world replete with its major components and pregnant with the symbolic power contained in the macrocosm. Each one of these components is of Celtic character and has a paradigm in ancient Irish myth.

We must remember, however, that despite the apparent universal nature

St. Caillin's Well, Ballyconneely, Co. Galway (33). Prehistoric
spiral bed where patterns are still done.

St. Lassair's Well, Lough Meelagh, Co. Roscommon (15).
An early stone table and stone under which backs are
healed and upon which a priest says Mass.

of these components grounded in myth, the fundamental power of each one comes not from the myth exclusively but from the situation or context in which it is found. It is the place of the tree, stone, or well, with its own particularity, that sets it apart from other places and renders it powerful. The Glen of Aherlow is different from Omey Island. Each has a spirit that resides there, arising from the feeling of the place, a *deus loci*. Further, each stone is different in shape or intention, one a menhir, one a table, one a bed or seat. The same distinction applies to the trees, one a thorn, one an ash, one a hazel; some with clooties, others with coins embedded within the trunk, still others of peculiar shapes but unadorned. The spring, too, contains power not only because it imitates the model of the Well of Segais in the myth but more properly because of its location and the property of its waters; one is by the sea and open to its tides, one flows from a rocky cleft on a mountainside, and another is at the center of a low-lying field. Still further, one may have a sacred fish living within it, one an eel, or one may contain never-ceasing bubbles that provide inspiration to the person who drinks from it.

In addition to the differences between each component from well to well and the differences in placehood from site to site, there is another point that adds to the loric nature of the holy wells. This is the fact that every well site does not always contain all the components. Thus out of a hundred sites we may find that half contain all three components, another third contain two of the components, and still other sites contain only one component, the spring, but also have a magical fish living in the spring. The well does not gain its power from a standardized set of components that repeat themselves at each site. Rather it is the site itself and the particularity of the components present there that radiate power, and this power is thus loric in nature. In order for the wells to be identified as sacred sites in all respects, they would have to be located in identical or similar contexts, and each would contain all three of the major components of the well complex. Further, the spirit that manifested itself there would have to be universally revered throughout the entire "world."

With the coming of Patrick and the intensification of Christianity, however, certain aspects of sacred power were manifested at the wells. This imposition of sacred power on the wells was a necessity that accompanied Christianity simply because Christianity, in its sacred nature, rests upon a constellation of symbols and myths that are universally revered throughout

Christendom. It is because of this universally recognized symbolism that we can speak of the Christian world. This world is not identified with a place but with the symbols, myths, and rituals that constitute the Christian tradition.

Certain loric phenomena at the wells, then, were revalorized in terms of the universal symbols of Christianity. At the same time, however, the power of the wells, whether consciously or unconsciously acknowledged, still sprang from the place and the particularity of the sanctions located there.

St. John the Baptist Well, Castlemahon, Co. Limerick (52). A well that has been universalized through dedication to a canonized saint.

4

The Coming of Patrick

Historical and Cosmic Worldviews

BEFORE WE DISCUSS Patrick and the transformation of loric springs to holy wells, we need to ponder the questions scholars have asked as to how the culture of an intruding power can be persuasive in the country intruded upon. Is it simply a matter of one power forcing its ways upon another as, for example, the British in India or the Spanish in Central and South America? Or is there a more subtle process taking place? Are there particular conditions necessary within the context of the invaded country that make possible some form of synthesis between the two traditions? We think that in order to proceed from one tradition to another, or from one mode of being to another, there must be certain symbolic conditions present that make possible the crossing of the boundary between the two cultures. In other words, there must be certain symbols that are shared between the two cultures, even though the interpretation of those symbols may differ or may take place on different levels within the horizon of those symbols' possible meanings.

To begin with, there are several factors that need to be considered in transformations which result in varying forms of cultural syncretism. We wish to use the word *syncretism* in a special way and to distinguish it from synthesis. Whereas we understand synthesis to be a result of the blending of two separate forms into a third or new form, syncretism retains both forms that gave rise to it in a harmonious and integrated way. Syncretism functions as an unresolved paradox, or what we would term a symbol.

In order to achieve a syncretic transformation, common symbolic constellations are necessary; this is the most important factor. In addition, the symbols must be recognizable from both cultural perspectives. Finally, the culture types involved must have some degree of commonality for any syncretism to occur. If these factors are not present, either the intrusive tradition will, in time, be absorbed completely by the home culture, or that indigenous culture will be completely annihilated by the intruder. Unlike this simple transformation, cultural syncretism requires a special set of conditions.

The conditions present at the juxtaposition of Irish Celtic and Christian cultures in the fifth century contained the ingredients necessary for cultural syncretism, but it was a syncretism that brought with it a change in the level of the interpretation of the symbol complex from the loric to the sacred. This change in level of interpretation was due to the difference in culture types within the two traditions. A hierophany, to use Eliade's term in its widest sense, is "anything which manifests the sacred," and the hierophany of the sky involves "high" gods, that is, gods who are above and who create and order what is and are generally unavailable or transcendent except through their representative(s). The closest place to this god would be a high place such as a mountain. The Sumerian ziggurat and the Indian Mount Meru are just two of the countless examples of a cosmic summit as center of the earth. Personal salvation would be attained by ascension, reaching upward to heaven. Ladders, steps, and rising paths are common means to attain access to a sky hierophany. The sky-god hierophany in which Christianity participates is characterized by particular rituals having to do with purification. Since all things come from above, water is placed upon the head and is sprinkled over people and objects much as rain that comes from the sky nourishes the earth. Immersion rituals such as baptism are seen as ritual death and regeneration. Symbols such as a cross or pole represent the *axis mundi*. Through penetration of the sky canopy, the other world may be attained. Those things that remain in the underworld symbolize darkness, chaos, and decay.

In contrast, the Irish Celtic tradition was cosmic in its orientation and perceived sacred power as originating and emanating from the earth. In fact, the focus on the earth was so intense that there was very little notion of a world in an expansive and all-encompassing sense. Thus, the power of the place was predominant over the power of world. The primary form of power present in Ireland, then, was the loric, which accompanies the elementary cosmic orientation. In such an orientation there are no urban centers seeking to extend their power and stressing the universalizing dimension of that power but rather a complex of decentralized villages, each with its own center and power site. Because of the connection of the Celts with a particular place and because of the subsistence level of their livelihood, there were few attempts made to expand landholdings into a large monolithic area that was total and could be conceived of as a world. Power instead was based upon the uniqueness of a place and its people.

The Christians, however, were bent upon expanding their already large world unto the ends of the earth. In addition, theirs was an urban religion with a well-organized hierarchy that encompassed the Christian world. Their god was in the sky and thus had a good "view" of the "world." Consequently, when the syncretism occurred between the Celtic and Christian cultures in Ireland, with the resulting appellation "Celtic Christianity," there was a shift in the level of power from the loric to the sacred. But this shift was a gradual one that took place in increments over the period from the coming of Patrick in A.D. 432 until the battle of the Boyne in 1690.

Despite the essential difference in cultures between the Christian and the Celtic, there were certain aspects of commonality. To begin with the most obvious, Christ was a cosmic figure who, like the Irish figure Cú Chulainn, disappears several times into the "other world," there to gain wisdom and expertise that he used upon his return to this world to "redeem" his enemies. Further, like the vegetation deities of ancient Egypt and Mesopotamia, Christ dies and rises again in imitation of the yearly cycle of plants. Finally, like the Celtic chieftain, Christ is identified with the sacred tree, in this case in the syncretic form of the cross. In addition, the Christian liturgical year follows the Celtic yearly seasonal procession in structure, having only a historical overlay imposed upon it. For example, both calendars end and begin at the nadir, not the zenith, of the solar cycle, and both also employ an overlay of lunar points upon the solar base; thus Easter is a lunar festival coming on the first Sunday after the first full moon after the vernal equinox.[1]

An additional similarity is that the Celts in Ireland, ostensibly at least, presented a cultural facade that was strongly patriarchal, one in which, as in other historical cultures, the warrior was held in great esteem. Further, there developed a warrior aristocracy that was hierarchical in the same way as the *ecclesia* of the Christian Church. In a very special way, then, Patrick's Christianity and Ireland's Celtic religion were two sides of the same coin, one emphasizing the cosmic, female dimension, the other the historical, male dimension.

Because of these overlaps in cultural typology between the Irish Celts and the Patrician Christians, there were certain symbolic constellations within the respective cultures that were common in structure but different in interpretation. But in spite of the differing emphases within the respective cultures, it was the common symbolic complexes that provided the conditions for the possibility of syncretism between Celt and Christian in Ireland. The process of the syncretism itself, made possible by the above conditions, seems to parallel in structure what Edmund Husserl in his discourses on phenomenology terms "the intentionality of consciousness."[2] Briefly put, intentionality describes the nature of the relationship established in consciousness between the subject whose consciousness it is and the object to which that consciousness reaches. The quality of this relationship is such that it incorporates both transcendence, or exteriority, and immanence, or interiority. In other words, as consciousness or the subject opens up through interest or fascination to the object within its reach, that object gives itself to that consciousness. The object actually enters into the consciousness of the subject; it becomes immanent to the subject. Despite this immanence, the object remains other, something other than the subject, and this presence of immanence and transcendence occurs simultaneously. There is a form of syncretism that occurs between the consciousness and that which presents itself to the consciousness, yet the articulation of this syncretism is intended or conveyed by and through the consciousness of the subject. However clearly and sympathetically consciousness may perceive or understand the other, it is always perceived and understood through the subjectivity of that particular consciousness. In this sense it is the intention of that particular consciousness. This syncretism of subject and object is made possible only by some commonality, no matter how obscured that commonality may be initially. It is through this common ground, which within phenomenology is termed "foreknowledge" or "foreconception," that the possibility of a genuine understanding of, and opening to, the other presents itself.

From the Loric to the Sacred:
Christianization of Symbols at the Wells

Let us now juxtapose this very general sketch of the intentional relationship between subject and object with the relationship that evolved between Celt and Christian in Ireland in the hope that each will shed light on the other. The holy well presents a microcosm of Ireland, a center at which were located certain symbolic complexes that met the earlier stated requirements. That is, there were certain symbols at the wells that had a common grounding in both Christian and Celtic traditions and that made possible the syncretism that occurred between them. The holy wells provide us with the crucible for that syncretism. It was at the well that Celt and Christian met, and there that the intentional relationship was established that resulted in the hybrid called Celtic Christianity, which later became a thorn in the side of Rome.

Let us explore some of the symbols that appear at the sacred springs of the Celts as loric themes and see how they could become sacred symbols for the Christians based upon a common grounding within the two traditions. Perhaps one of the most striking of these bridge symbols is that of the fish. There are many wells about which the loric theme of a fish dwelling in the well presents itself. Recall the tale told us by Mary Costello about the golden trout she saw on the eve of her wedding as well as the story of her friend Ellen Walsh, who also saw the sacred trout and was cured of lameness. When we asked Mrs. Costello what she thought the trout was, she replied that she guessed it was the saint. It is Saint Eoin's Well in Listowel, County Kerry, in which this trout lives. But we were also told of a white trout living in St. Brigid's Well in Liscannor, County Clare (45). This tale was told to us by our taxi driver, Francis McTigue from Ennis, County Clare, whose sister it was who saw the trout. A variation on the theme is found at St. Michael's Well at Balleymore West, County Kerry (46). Here a small eel dwells in the well. According to one source who saw the eel, it is about four inches long and is colored a greenish brown. Two other sources told our investigator that the eel had been taken from the well in a bucket of water and that the water would not boil. When the eel was returned to the well and another bucket of water was taken, it boiled.

According to Celtic mythology a sacred salmon dwelled in the Other-world in the Well of Segais, the model for all surface sacred springs. The red spots on the sides of the salmon were caused by the magical berries (nuts) of the nearby hazel tree falling into the water. Together, the berries and the water conveyed to the salmon the magical wisdom present in the water of the well. Whoever would eat the salmon would gain this wisdom. The salmon was also associated with the hero of the *Táin Bó Cuailnge*, Cú Chulainn, one of whose magical feats was his great salmon leap. Finn was the recipient of wisdom from the salmon when he was cooking it for his teacher. Thus, the salmon is the bearer of transformative wisdom, the wisdom known as sovereignty, the intuitive wisdom given the chieftain by the goddess at the time of his inauguration. This meaning is retained in the holy wells of today, but now the fish heals. Yet healing is a form of wisdom, a coming together of things that are not by nature separated but that, through injury, have been rent apart. In the present context the fish has been transformed from the person of the chieftain to that of the saint to whom the well is dedicated.

How does the Christian share in this salmonoid symbolism? As far back as the second century, the fish has been used in Christian iconography as a symbol of Christ's being. A specific iconography was used to convey this symbolism that incorporated the Greek letters ΙΧΘΥΣ, which form the word for *fish*. The letters of the word stand for Jesus Christ, God's son, Savior. Thus the fish bore for Christians an occult symbolism that bound them together as one body. The image of the fish proceeded to take on the symbolism of Christ himself.

Another association of the fish in early Christianity was with baptism and the newly baptized. In this case the initiates were identified with fish (Christ) and referred to as *pisciculi*, little fishes. The baptismal font itself was called a *piscina*, or fishpond.[3] Even the Eucharist itself was identified symbolically with the fish, in accordance with Christ's relationship to the fish.[4] Each of these symbols was a reflection of mythic models established in the Scriptures. The Old Testament presents the image of the cosmic fish in the tale of Jonah and the whale. Here the fish is the world mother who gives a new life to Jonah through his symbolic death in her belly and his later disgorgement, alive and renewed. In the New Testament life is again associated with the fish and with Jesus. Recall the well-known passage of the feeding of the five thousand in the Gospels. Here again the fish plays the role of life-giving and fertile mother, able miraculously to feed five thousand people with just two fish. This miraculous fecundity is reminiscent of the magical cow in the tales preceding the *Táin* who in one milking was able to feed all the men in Ireland. Certainly we are dealing in both cases with feminine, earth-centered symbols of fecundity and life renewal.

Just as the biblical fish present symbols of fecundity and rebirth, so, too, the wisdom of the salmon in the well is a watery wisdom that heals and brings with it a complete renewal. Finally, is not the baptismal font, the *piscina,* or fishpond, symbolically homologous with the sacred spring of Celtic Ireland? Both are containers of "fish," and both are bringers of new life and fertility.

But there is one more important factor peculiar to the salmon, the eel, and Jesus that is decisive in providing the possibility for a syncretism between Celt and Christian. Let us begin with a symbolic examination of the salmon. What is distinctive about the salmon in relationship to other fish is that it lives in the sea but leaves the sea and enters a freshwater river to mate. In other words, the salmon is a boundary crosser, which by crossing the boundary is able to bring about transformation and new life. Further, the boundary crossed is from salt to fresh water, symbolically from the feminine to the masculine, from earth to sky. It is also important to note that the river to which the salmon returns is the place of its birth.

The eel is also a crosser of boundaries. It, too, moves from salt to fresh water and back again, but the process is in the reverse order to the salmon. Thus, the eel spends most of its time in fresh water, then at night crawls on its belly across the land to the sea off the Bermuda Islands where it breeds. The origin of the eel is in the sea, the salmon in the rivers. The salmon in accordance with its place of origin is masculine, the eel feminine, and together they form the totality of the gods. Both eel and salmon are mercurial figures, bringers of transformation, wisdom, and life.

With the coming of Christianity, the fish at the well became identified indirectly with Christ, but more directly with a saint. Syncretism had taken place between Celtic and Christian symbols based upon a common cosmic ground, but at the same time the symbol was transformed from the loric to the sacred. In other words, through the Christianization of the well, the sacred fish dwelling in the well was cut loose from its roots in the particular place and catapulted into universal status. The sacrality of the well could now be recognized and understood anywhere within the Christian world. Thus, wherever we find a St. John's Well or a St. Michael's, Margaret's, or Joseph's Well, we witness the vertical process of transformation from place to world, from particular to universal. To be sure, this process takes place in a minority of wells, for most of them, through Christianization, have taken the name of a local saint, often not on the officially canonized roll of Rome. In many cases the Irish saint in question has assumed a conglomerate of the names of ancient chieftains who at one time ruled in the *tuath* in which the well is located.[5]

One more example will suffice to establish clearly the possibility of syncretism between Celt and Christian at the sacred springs. Next to the symbol of Christ, the most important image within the Christian tradition is the cross. In early tradition the cross of Christ that appears at the end of the "old age" is identical with the Tree of Life that was established at the beginning of time. Eliade reminds us that the wood of the true cross has the power to bring the dead to life. "The wood had this power because the cross was made out of the Tree of Life which stood in the Garden of Eden."[6] Thus, Jesus is the "man hung on the Tree," and through his contact with the Tree of Life, all humankind will be brought back to life, that is, will be given new life. In this symbolism Christ took on the sin of all humankind through his suffering, passion, and death on the tree. In fact he becomes identified not only with the sin of humankind but with sin itself. By hanging on the Tree of Life, sin becomes purified, transformed into new life that is eternal in the same sense that the Garden of Eden is eternal.

This cross/tree symbolism bridges easily to the Celtic symbol of the *bile,* or the sacred tree that stood by the well. For this tree, too, was a tree of life in the broadest sense of the symbol. It, too, through its connection to the ancestors and the Otherworld, takes the chieftain or devotee at the well back to the beginning of time and the Otherworld, the Celtic version of the Garden of Eden. An even clearer symbolic bridge is found in the practice of tying clooties, or small bits of cloth or clothing, onto the *bile.* Here the clooties, because of intimate contact with the wearer, contain the pain, the illness, the sin, or the brokenness of the supplicant. They are placed upon the tree and left there so that they will be in constant contact with the source of life represented by the ancestors and present in the tree. Thus the *bile* takes upon itself the accumulated sin and illness of all in the parish, or in earlier times, the *tuath.* This truly is the sin of the world, for the *tuath,* the place, was the equivalent of the world before modern times.

We have seen sacred trees at such wells as St. Patrick's in Ballyshannon,

79

St. Brigid's Well, Killaire, Co. Westmeath (55). A typical
example of the rock, tree, water complex found at many
holy wells.

County Donegal, and Doon Well near Kilmacrennan, County Donegal, that were so laden with clooties that one could not see the trees' branches. It was an eerie sight and gave forth the image of a dead man wrapped in funerary bandages. At Doon Well the tree was very small, barely a few feet tall, and was bent over severely by its burden, as though it was truly taking on the sickness of the entire world.

Both *bile* and cross are healers of a broken humanity, separated from the wholeness of the goddess or from God. When Celt and Christian met at the well, the sacred tree present there became a bridge over which the two could walk to join hands in a common symbolism, a symbolism uniting them in a bond that resulted in the Celtic Christian tradition. Some of the primary symbols that made this unity possible, that enabled the mutual acceptance through understanding of Celt and Christian, resided at the holy well. The well, the center of Irish Celtic spiritual life, became the hidden ground of Celtic Christianity and remains today a primary source that joins together for the people of Ireland their church and their land.

The Power of Patrick

Who then was Patrick, the Christian evangelist about whom we have so little actual historical data, and yet who had such a profound and enduring influence upon the Irish despite his apparent opposition to the Celtic cosmic hierophany? Our chief source is *The Tripartite Life of Patrick*,[7] a compendium of Patrician information from various ancient manuscript sources, including the Book of Armagh, a ninth-century manuscript, which is filled with descriptions of Patrick's activities at venerated springs. Our interest in Patrick need not be concerned with the annalistic evidence of his chronology, his actual existence in history, or with the arguments concerning the possibility of two Patricks. Those arguments can best be addressed by historians. However, evidence of the Patrician influence upon rituals at the venerated springs found both in the early writings and in the practices that persist at these wells right into the present time is of great interest. It seems clear that his genius influenced the meaning and use of those sites and transformed them from venerated springs to holy wells.

Although Patrick is generally thought to be a Roman missionary Christian, what is important here is that he spent his adolescence in slavery in Ireland as a herder and later escaped into Gaul. His understanding of the Irish Celtic character, then, was probably unusually extensive for a Roman Catholic of that time, even including those Romans who had preceded him to the missions in Ireland. Bishop Germanus sent him to follow Palladius, first bishop to the Irish Christians, in spite of what some of the British synod considered to be his unsuitability.[8] Their objections to his appointment as bishop of Ireland had to do with his semiliteracy, the result of his years in captivity, and the dangers of violence from the heathen Irish. The qualities Patrick brought to his mission were a direct result of those privations he had suffered in his slavery. He arrived in Ireland with a previously acquired experiential understanding of the so-called heathen ways of the Irish in the early fifth century. This empathy with the indigenous people seems to have been one reason why Patrick's influence was so much greater than that of the precursory monks. Another determining factor in favor of his influence and success perhaps lay in an ancient prophecy, preceding his arrival, which said:

> Across the sea will come Adze Head
> Crazed in the head
> His cloak with a hole for the head.[9]

Stone heads in prehistoric usage were associated with the wells, and we can see how the prophecy was an opening for Patrick with his shaved tonsure and flowing robes to appear as a compassionate incarnation of the pagan stone god who was "Blood Crusted, insatiable, [and] to him without glory would they sacrifice their firstborn with wailing and danger pouring new blood for the stooped one."[10] Patrick's legendary influence was powerful and immediate as he marked out safe boundaries against the old stone powers. As a shape-shifter and magician, Patrick practiced his craft in countless contests with the druids, demonstrating that his power was greater than any seen before. At one meeting Patrick is said to have appeared in white robes, reading with druids at Oglalla Well. White is a druidic color, and one would expect Patrick to have been wearing brown. His powerful shape-shifting ability is told in a passage in the *Tripartite Life* called "The Song of the Deer." As the tale goes, Patrick was trying to elude the men sent out by King Leogaire of Tara to kill him. Patrick's offense had been to light the paschal fire on a nearby hill before the king had exercised his prerogative to light the first fire of Beltaine. "Thereafter went Patrick and his train of eight . . . past all ambushes in the shape of eight deer and behind them one fawn with a white bird on its shoulder."[11] These are but a few examples of the abilities that enabled him to convert the power of the venerated spring to a holy well.

Legends also abound concerning Patrick's rejection of hags, giving us clues about Patrick's conversion activity at the wells. The earliest tale occurs shortly after his arrival in Ireland. He is offered a staff by an eternal black hag, the "daughter" of a young couple he met by the sea. He refuses to accept this staff, saying that he prefers to wait to take up a staff that will be offered to him by God at a later date.[12] Indeed, the *Bachall Ísu,* as this staff was called, was acquired by Patrick and was used in many transformative activities at the springs that he visited all over Ireland. For instance, Patrick "marked out with his crozier a cross in the flagstones and cut the stone as if it were soft clay."[13] Many further marks of Patrick are found on stones he knelt on, in stone beds he slept in, and in various other permanent signs. He often created new wells with the *Bachall Ísu* as he circumambulated Ireland in imitation of the king's circuit. As he sained the wells with his staff, he purified them from snakes and underworld creatures; the hags were destroyed, and the waters were consecrated to the sky-god. Often Patrick would rename the well for himself. For example, a site called Tullaghan Well, which is said to have been the habitat of the last snake and is known to be of pre-Patrician origin, was rededicated to St. Patrick, who prayed for a drink, causing the well to "spring up." A head (*gamh*) was kept in the water, which turned it bitter, but it now alternates between fresh and bitter.[14] Tullaghan Well, at the northeast end of the Ox Mountain range in County Sligo, has connections with the festival of Lughnasa, a pre-Christian ritual associated with the Celtic god Lug. Remnants of this patron fair and rounds still exist and were still being attended in the second half of this century. The well is currently being visited and holds claim to many cures. Another site in Dromard, a St. Patrick's well (47), is said to be "the oldest in Connaught." According to a local tourist pamphlet called *The History of Sligo,* water from this well was used to purify and consecrate all the other holy wells in the province of Connaught. Another example of a sained well is at Aughris (48); a well there associated with the Celtic king Muiredach (a Lughnasa well) is now dedicated to St. Patrick. Numerous other wells were struck or newly created on the earth by Patrick with a blow of his staff. Patrick's power came down from the sky-god through his staff

Tober Oglalla, Tulsk, Co. Roscommon (12). Location of
the conversion of the pagan twins by St. Patrick.

Tober Oglalla, Tulsk, Co. Roscommon (12). View of
artifacts considered sacred at this site.

Bachall Ísu to purify the water of the wells, in a sense to invert the Celtic power of the "ale" (heavy fecundating brew). In Christian use the water was holy but did not have the power of the sacred spring of knowledge. Patrick flies in upon the wells, driving down upon the earthly power, dislodging what was there. He is said to be carried on "seven-league boots" as he thrusts his staff into the wells in a tireless circuit about the whole of Ireland.

A striking example of the holy well as matrix for the syncretism of Celt and Christian is found in *The Tripartite Life of Saint Patrick*. The tale begins in the following manner: "Hereafter Patrick went at sunrise to the well, namely, Cliabach on the sides of Cruachan. The clerics sat down by the well. Two daughters of Loegaire son of Niall went early to the well to wash their hands, as was a custom of theirs, namely, Ethne the Fair and Fedelm the Ruddy."[15] These sentences tell us a great deal about the context and use of the holy well both during and before Patrick's coming to Ireland. This particular well, Cliabach, is the sacred spring that is part of the royal site of the province of Connaught called Cruachan. We can see that it was an active place, visited daily by the royal household for various purposes. It was also a place for contemplation and healing due to its identification with the goddess. Patrick must have known that wells were such places and that he would find there both royalty and holy men with whom he could discourse.

His visit to Cliabach was no exception, for there arrived at the well two druids, here called wizards, Moel and Caplait. They were affiliated with the royal site, for the tale mentions that Caplait had fostered Fedelm. In the course of the meeting Patrick baptizes the girls and later, because of their extreme zeal to see Christ, lets them die. "And they asked to see Christ face to face. And Patrick said to them: 'Ye cannot see Christ unless ye first taste of death, and unless ye receive Christ's Body and his Blood.' And the girls answered: 'Give us the sacrifice that we may be able to see the Spouse.' Then they received the sacrifice, and fell asleep in death; and Patrick put them under one mantle in one bed; and their friends bewailed them greatly."[16]

This striking event at the well establishes the intimate and blood-sealed bond that was forged, not without resistance, between Celt and Christian. Two forms of sacrificial death were combined to forge the bond, one Christian, one Celtic. The first was the death through water by baptism in the well, and the second the death through blood by human sacrifice. It was a relationship in which one died in order to allow the other to give itself face to face. But this death was not one-sided, for it was accomplished at and through the well. Thus the Celtic well, vagina of the goddess, accepts within her the Christian death by watery baptism. The two traditions have merged, but they have done so through the subjectivity of the Christian, Patrick. Later in the tale, that syncretism completes itself when the druids, Moel and Caplait, are converted by Patrick.

This conversion could not have happened without a common symbolism, overt or covert. In this case both traditions were grounded in the symbols of death and rebirth, one for the sake of history and the other for the sake of the cosmos. Further, both revere the confluence of blood and water as instruments for this transformation. It was blood and water that flowed from Christ's side as he hung dying on the cross, and it was blood and water that flowed from Queen Medb's vagina as she lay defeated after the last battle in *Táin Bó Cuailnge*.[17] In the first case humankind is reborn through the taking of this blood and water in the rituals of the Eucharist and baptism; and in the second the sacred rivers Boyne and Shannon are said to have come from Medb's "gush of blood," and from the rivers the Irish people are reborn.

This relationship is intentional. As Christ becomes immanent in Ethne and Fidelm through their willing death, so the Celtic spring becomes immanent in Patrick's acceptance and use of it in baptism. Both Celt and Christian see one another as different, but through a setting aside of self they have enabled the other to dwell within them. What results is a syncretism that announces itself as Christian but is nurtured by the sweet and healing waters of the Celtic spring, the goddess herself. Celtic Christianity amounted to a "seeing" of Celtic symbols through the subjectivity of a Christian. At least this remained the case until the Synod of Whitby in 664 when Roman ways were forced upon the Celts.

5

From Brigid to Mary

Deus Loci *to National Saint*

IN OUR STUDY OF the holy wells over the past decade we have attempted to focus not only on the continuity of symbolism present at the well from prehistoric times to the present but also on the shift in emphasis from the wells of St. Brigid to those of the Blessed Virgin Mary. This gradual but certain movement is not simply a shift from one female saint to another but a shift in the ground of power from the loric to the sacred. While St. Brigid is of local origin and continuous with the earlier Celtic goddess Brigid, the Virgin Mary, as the Mother of God, is present throughout the entire Christian world. Thus, we are presented in her being with an example of a world-building symbol that is universalizing in its power.

Let us review, for a moment, the notion of the *deus loci* and its connection with the power of the loric. Loric power is the power of place and is tied to the earth in its particularity, in its unique configurations and subterranean power at a particular place. The *deus loci* is the deity of a particular place; as such it is the "spirit" of the place in a double sense. It is the feeling of unique power that one experiences in a particular place, and it is the spirit abstracted from that place or thematized in the form of a supernatural being. Thus, the deity of Aherlow Glen may be known only to those people residing in that glen and is sacred only to them. In a way, the *deus loci* marks off the boundaries of the place and of the people residing there. The presence of this deity establishes the horizon of the sociogeographical region. Growing out of these ontological horizons are the village boundaries and the boundaries of cultivated and uncultivated land.

To be sure, all the land within the precincts of a given *deus loci* is full of loric power, but some spots within the place are more powerful than others. This is because these spots are places of conjunction between surface and subterranean power. For example, on the surface of the earth, one might find a spring bounded by a large stone and tree. Here it is the configuration of the earth that provides the particularity of loric power. But why are some springs revered while others are not? Our conjecture is that the reason lies in the conjunction beneath the spring of two forms of energy lines. One form of energy or power is contained in subterranean veins of water that shift direction beneath the earth's surface due to contact with immutable substances such as clay or impervious rock. The other type of power is in the form of beams of earth energy that run in straight lines. Where these beams of earth energy cross the water vein as it rises to the surface, we find a healing or transforming power. The two forms of subterranean power, then, one straight, one meandering, represent opposing qualities that Sig Lonegren in his book *Spiritual Dowsing* compares to the Chinese *yang* and *yin*, or male and female energies. Lonegren states, "This Earth of ours . . . has always had a series of places all over her surface where the *yin* and *yang*, the female and male, the domes and veins of primary water and the straight energy leys have come together forming what is called a 'power center.'"[1] In Celtic symbolism we are presented in such a power center with the mating of the chieftain and the goddess, which is reflected on the surface by the sacred trout in the well and by the ritual of inauguration of the chieftain, in which he mates with the "place."

To summarize, wells are holy because of a *coincidentia oppositorum* or coming together of power types on various levels at the same time. On the surface of the earth we are presented with the break in space, which is the well itself with its striking configuration. Within the well is the sacred fish uniting with and living through the water, while around the well the chieftain, at the proper break in time, unites with the goddess by imbibing the water of the well. The well provides access to the Otherworld beneath the surface where we find mated the primordial source of the surface structure in the crossing of energy leys and primary water, represented mythologically in the Celtic realm by the Lord of the Otherworld and his consort, the Earth Goddess. Where these various levels are functioning simultaneously and reflecting each other, we have a potential holy well; where they are not, we have simply a spring in a lovely setting. The loric site within the place, then, is a reflection of what is taking place beneath the surface of the earth. This notion is in complete agreement with the mythic cosmology of ancient Ireland in which power is generated beneath the earth, moves upward, and is there reflected in the rituals and social structure of the *tuath*.

What, then, is it that precipitates the shift from the self-enclosed organism of the place to the ever-expanding plane of the world; from the particularizing and self-reflective space of the loric to the universalizing and projective world of the sacred? Something foreign must be introduced into the self-enclosed placehood of the loric in much the same way as a grain of sand is introduced into an oyster. Like the pearl that results from that irritation, a new and syncretic form of power that is world-creating radiates from the encounter.

The grain of sand that was introduced into the placehood of ancient Ireland was Christianity, which not only is impelled by the power of the sacred but is a historical religion bent upon the expansion of its own way through the process of history. Because the nature of Christianity is grounded in the sacred, it has a universalizing tendency that attempts to convert or absorb those cultural forms that are counter to its own. Because Christianity is a historical religion, it is compelled to be mobile, carrying with it wherever it goes the tools of its revelation, which are reflected in the vastness of the sky and which clash with the coziness of the earth.

The Roman world out of which Christianity came was dependent upon and manifested vastness and uniformity, characteristics of the sky in which the Christian god was believed to dwell. In contemporary terms Christianity functioned in ancient Ireland as television did in Appalachia; it was a mass medium that introduced certain universalizing symbols that broke the self-contained and decentralized circles that harbored the loric power as a mother holds her child.

One of the major factors contributing to the breakdown of the loric is that of labor migration. In other words, occupational forms that are unrelated to the ecology of the situation are introduced. The introduction of these discontinuous forms acts as an irritant that throws off the ecological balance of labor. An example of labor migration out of balance within the context of the Irish Celtic world is the introduction of celibate priests. Over time, the priest or monk in Ireland supplanted the local chieftain as the monastery supplanted the *tuath*. The occupation of the priest, however, was out of balance with that of the chieftain in that he was antithetical to the promotion of the fecundity and renewal of the earth as goddess. In his celibate role his job was that of purification through discrimination rather than renewal through integration. The latter role was attached to the Irish chieftain in his relationship to the *deus loci*.

As a result of this occupational imbalance coupled with the universalizing nature of Christianity and its emphasis on world and the sacred, the role of the *deus loci* was replaced by that of the Christian saint. The saint represented the world as a whole in varying degrees and levels. For example, on the level closest to the loric we find saints such as St. Peakaun. Although St. Peakaun is a Christian saint, his power is tacitly derived from the place in which he "resides" and in which his hermitage is located. This place, Aherlow Glen in County Tipperary, is not well known or large. In so far as St. Peakaun had power, the place had power. Thus his power is at base loric, though it was melded with the sacred to the extent that it became lodged within the Christian Church. The various saints with the name of Finn are another illustration of the connection with place. St. Finnian of Moville came from a place called Drum Finn. St. Dublitter Finn was from Finglass while St. Fintan was from Findrum and St. Finnian of Clonard from Ros Findchuill, the original name of Clonard.[2] Each of these places of origin is the name for some natural form that was the giver of power to the place and thence to the saint. Drum Finn means "fair ridge," Finglass means "bright or fair stream," and Ros Find-chuill means "promitory of the fair wood."

A second level of synthesizing the loric with the sacred occurs in saints such as Brigid or Finntan. Both these figures are important in Irish myth associated with the whole of Ireland, but not with the entirety of the Christian world. It is interesting to note that there are three saints named Finntan listed in John Delaney's *Dictionary of Saints*.[3]

Finally, we find saints who are universal within the Christian world and clearly gain the majority of their power from the sacred; but being located at holy wells, they continue to draw somewhat from the power of place, the loric. Examples of such wells are St. Margaret's Well, County Clare (49); St.

St. Margaret's Well, Ennis/Kilrush Road, Co. Clare (49).
An example of a universalized well with a crossed circle,
symbol of Celtic and Christian syncretism.

St. Augustine's Well, Kilshanny, Co. Clare (50). A well
that has been universalized through dedication to a
canonized saint.

Augustine's Well, Kilshanny, County Clare (50); St. John's Well, Warrenstown, County Meath (51); and St. John the Baptist Well, Castlemahon, County Limerick (52). The wells of the universal saints are clearly in the minority, thus the power of the loric remains a potent force within the overall syncretism of Christian and Celtic traditions in Ireland.

The figure of the saint at the well is an emblem of the multivalent power present at the well since the coming of Patrick. Despite the process of Christianization or universalization that continues to take place in Ireland, there is retained within the symbol of the holy well a loric root that functions as the "collective unconscious" of the symbol. Its power filters up into the conscious symbol, the saint, the well water, and the place, in a manner that, for the most part, is unacknowledged and often taken for granted.

Loric and Sacred, Orectic and Normative

The model that we have been setting forth to understand the nature of the holy well is in a certain sense three-dimensional. There is a process moving through time from the loric to the sacred that has no depth of its own. Yet, occurring at each moment of that process is a variable integration of the sacred and the loric, an integration in which the balance of the two forms of power shifts in relation to the point on the process line. It is this shift in the balance of power that provides the depth or third dimension to the model.

Further amplification of this notion is present in the work of Victor and Edith Turner. They also have explored the syncretism of ancient Irish and Christian traditions located at pilgrimage sites in Ireland, and their work provides a similar model for understanding this syncretism, but on a different scale. The difference in scale and terms provides a space for complementary meanings to arise.

In contrast to the notions of the loric and the sacred, which are primarily distinguished by the type and quality of space, the Turners present a polarity that is distinguished by differing attitudes of consciousness. Thus, our focus in the use of the sacred and the loric is upon the "great" or exterior world, while the focus of the Turners is upon the "little" or interior world that occurs within the psyche of the individual. Taken together, these thoughts provide a holistic understanding of the holy well and its context, both geographical and psychological, that incorporates a concern for the place in which the well appears, the people who are in relationship to the well in that place, and the transformations that take place at the site through time.

The notion employed by the Turners is set forth in a polarity denoted by two terms, the "normative" and the "orectic." The content of these terms seems to provide a parallel to the sacred and the loric, at least in terms of their essence. At the base of each term are certain attitudes of consciousness. The normative or ideological pole is described as containing "ideals, values, legal principles, norms of social structure and theological doctrines," and "ethical imperatives of a general kind, of the Great Tradition."[4] These are the attitudes of world creation, the attitudes of a universalizing consciousness that parallels the power of the sacred but is placed within the sphere of the psyche. These attitudes then manifest themselves in society, which attempts, upon their basis, to establish an "ideological communitas" that is derived from nation or church and is universally valid.

While the general tenor of the normative pole is cerebral and lodged in thought, that of the orectic is emotional and grounded in feeling and sensory objects. The Turners describe the orectic as containing "objects, activities, relationships, ideas that arouse emotion and desire, feeling and willing." They are "highly localized, culturally specific objects and ideas . . . always being more closely related to the outward, sensorially perceptible form of the symbol."[5] In their discussion of the Irish Lough Derg pilgrimage known as St. Patrick's Purgatory, the Turners associate the pre-Christian artifacts at the site with the orectic pole and suggest that these symbols stimulate responses far beneath the surface of the normative order, reaching to the core of the archaic Irish character and even going to the deepest strata of the human psyche. "Strong emotions going back to childhood are generated by these symbols, indeed by their very archaism, to which may respond archaic psychological processes of the human psychobiological organism." In a sense, the orectic, like the loric, is grounded upon archaic universals manifested through cultural particularity and place. Further, the orectic field is the ground from which the normative emerges.[6] In psychological terms the orectic represents the unconscious modality, and the normative reflects the conscious modality.

This model implies also a movement or flow from orectic to normative, a flow that parallels on the psychic level the movement from loric to sacred.

Simultaneous with this flow is the copresence of the two poles at all points of the process. The Turners add that because of this copresence the two poles influence one another, bringing about the syncretism that we have referred to as Celtic Christianity. The Turners use the psychological term "transference" to describe this phenomenon, and they state that due to the "repetitive activity of ritual a transference may well be effected between semantic values of the two poles in the psyche of the actor, depending on how completely he enters the 'flow' of the ritual process. At Lough Derg it is entirely probable that Catholic ideas and doctrines become impregnated with Irish experiences, not only personal experiences but communitas experiences in an Irish landscape and culture setting, while specific symbols and ideas of Irishness, including that of being a persecuted people, are correspondingly Catholicized."[7]

The Turners provide a depth to the model of understanding that we have been setting forth, relating it specifically to the human psyche and its interpretation of its world. What results is an understanding of the relationship between Celt and Christian in Ireland that is not simply historical in a linear evolutionary sense. We must rather understand the movement from Celtic *tuath* to Christian world not as a line but as a spiral. The image of the spiral presents a process while at the same time providing a sense of depth. In each successive circle of the spiral the past repeats itself, lending a visual depth to the line, and presenting the archetype or model through the disguise of a more highly refined symbol system. As the spiral is a graphic synthesis of the line and the circle, so Celtic Christianity is a synthesis of the orectic and the normative, the loric and the sacred.

The "Spiraled History" of the Wells

The process and model of development about which we have been speaking can be seen in clear perspective in the history of the holy wells of Ireland, especially in its most recent history. The modern history of the wells presents an erosion of the loric base of the wells, a base in which the wells were tied completely to a place and to a national, if not local, saint. In the place of this has arisen a body of "universal" or sacred personages in the form of Catholic saints known throughout Christendom.

This double movement from loric to sacred and from orectic to normative can be illustrated by looking at the process taking place between the wells of St. Brigid and those of the Blessed Virgin Mary. Since the beginning of our study in 1979 we have noticed a definite sense of inertia and often of atrophy in the condition and use of the St. Brigid wells. We speak in a general or essential manner, for there remain certain very active sites of St. Brigid. Interesting also is the apparently reciprocal influence of the emerging and reactivated Marian wells on the Brigid wells as well as the influence of Brigid on the Virgin Mary.

St. Bridget is most probably a Christianization of the earlier Irish mother goddess Brigid or Brigit. She was the daughter/lover/wife of the Dagda, one of the Otherworld lords. Thus Brigid was the Otherworld queen renowned for powers of fertility and healing and for her patronage of the smith's fire and the arts of wisdom and poetry. She was especially identified with milk, dairy products, and the cow, as well as with sheep.

Irish folklore abounds with material concerning Brigid as a generous provider of cows, milk, butter, and cheese. At Belcoe, County Fermanagh, water changes to milk, and milk is poured upon the hills as an oblation.[8] In Balla butter was thrown into the water of the holy well. In the cult legends of Brigid, she was reared by a great red-eared Otherworld cow, and much legendary material connects her to dairy activities.[9] Brigid as a triple goddess, an androgynous figure, is both the eternal cauldron of the Dagda and also his daughter. She is the forerunner of such goddesses as Anu, Donn, and Danu[10] and is associated with fertility and plenty. She serves as mother of all. The "Vision of Mac Conglinne" gives us a wonderful satirical image of Brigid's generosity:

> The fort we reached was beautiful
> Thick breastworks of custard
> Above the lake
> Fresh butter for the drawbridge
> A moat of wheaten bread
> Walls of cheese curd
> Sleek pillars of ripe cheese
> And fleshed bacon posts
> In alternate rows;

Fine beams of yellow cream
Thin rafters of white spice
Hold up the house.
Spurting behind, a spring of wine
Beer and ale flowing in streams
And tasty pools; From a well-head of nectar
A crest of creamy malt ran
Over the floor.[11]

Here is a description of the mother of all, root goddess, the one who, in addition to her fertility, is the giver of an earthly wisdom that is the source of sovereignty and is contained in the intoxicating beverages found flowing in the chronicle. Her Christianization continued much of this symbolism, maintaining the same forms and meanings but historicizing them and placing them within a Christian symbolic and iconic context. She continued to be associated with the earth, and particularly the earth of Ireland, and thus became known as the Mary of the Gaels. She carried on the Earth Goddess symbolism in her continued association with water and especially with springs, eternally flowing sources of fertility, wholeness, and healing. Thus many holy wells are dedicated to her and often contain several dimensions of her power.

Later Christian tales emphasize a different Brigid, where we find a movement from fertile promiscuous goddess to a chaste and virginal saint. Her power is no longer derived from her intimacy with kings but from her transcendence, her virginal distance. The great paps are superseded by the notion of modesty. At least two instances of this may be found in legends in which Brigid is admonished to marry.[12] In both cases a youth compliments Brigid for her beautiful eyes, so she plucks one out and offers it to him! By this act she becomes ineligible to marry. In the first instance her guardian retrieves the eye and claps it back into its socket, promising not to force Brigid to marry anyone. In the second instance the admiring youth finds the dripping eye entirely repulsive and runs away. Brigid then heals herself by bathing the orbit in a holy well. Presumably the word gets around so that she is no longer approached by eligible swains, and her virginity remains inviolate from that time on.

Now let us begin our survey of her well at Kildare, the fifth-century site of her monastery and the repository of her sacred fire, tended by nine (some-times nineteen) virgins of her order. This site clearly maintains much of the early mother goddess symbolism, especially that of her relationship to the Lord of the Otherworld as divine smith and lord of the oak grove. The well is located just outside the town of Kildare and is dedicated to St. Brigid (53). This is her country, her place, and the well in 1984 was refurbished by local nuns. There are several unique features of this well that link St. Bridget to the goddess Brigid and thus to the place and the power of the loric. Near the spring itself, which is located on the edge of a field, is a stone tablet standing upright. On one side is incised a St. Bridget's cross, whose swastika form symbolizes the fiery sun and retains continuity with the goddess's association with the sacred smith and his fire. On the other side is incised a Christian cross, bringing together or syncretizing the loric and the sacred. But there is another stone image that seems forcefully to stress the loric roots of Brigid in the earth and especially in fertility as manifest through cows. As the water flows from the spring toward the glass-enclosed statue of the saint, it passes into and through two stone tubes and out their other ends. The tubes bring to mind the breasts of a woman, and the water flows through them as milk passes from the nipples of the Great Goddess to her children. There is noth-ing Christian to mollify this symbolism. In field interviews we were told that the stone tubes are called variously the "shoes" or "cows" of the saint. Ritual use of this well seems to have atrophied, for when the well was investigated in 1981 there was no pattern day and it had been superseded in ritual use by Father Moore's Well (54) located nearby. Iohannis Moore (d. 1826), accused by his bishop of using supernatural means of cures, is said to have breathed upon two candles, which ignited, and no one could blow them out. The bishop then exonerated him. A relic chimney-pot hat, kept by the Forde fam-ily, activated the well until it "disappeared" in recent times.

What we find at the ancient cult center of Brigid today is that this Earth Goddess of Kildare has metamorphosed into a Christian saint, St. Bridget, who has retained in her attributes and cult objects, including her well, many of her previous powers. She remains present in the earth, through which she heals by means of her holy well outside the town; and at that well we see the confluence of the symbolisms of fecundity, nurturing, and healing through the identification of milk and water as the spring flows through the stone "cows."

Father Moore's Well, Kildare, Co. Kildare (54). Pilgrim
seeks healing at this highly developed well.

The text on the stone reads:

THE BLESSED WELL OF FR. MOORE

FATHER JOHN MOORE, WAS
BORN IN 1779, AND RESIDED
HERE. HE WAS ORDAINED
AT MAYNOOTH, ABOUT 1803
AND WAS CURATE IN THE
PARISH OF ALLEN, HE DIED
ON THE 12TH MARCH 1826
AGED 47 YEARS.
HE WAS BURIED AT ALLEN.

FR. MOORE'S WONDERFUL
POWER IS SHOWN BY THE
MANY CURES AND FAVOURS
OBTAINED BY THOSE WHO
CARRY OUT THE STATIONS
AND TRADITIONAL PRAYERS
AT THE WELL.

Father Moore's Well, Kildare, Co. Kildare (54). This well is one that was activated by the priest's hat.

But much of her power has become dormant. There is no longer an active pattern or round at the well. This is not because well worship in general has declined, for Father Moore's Well nearby has gained in popularity and use in recent years, probably because Father Moore played a role that is closer to the people in mediation than the ancient St. Brigid. But the dormancy at Brigid's well is not in the form of unkemptness, because the well has recently been refurbished. The placing of the statue of St. Brigid behind glass at that time is emblematic of the type of dormancy that has occurred. Her power has been closed off from the people by a transparent shield. She has become a transcendent power manifest through an imposed neatness and order, more in the sense of a garden than as the powers of nature displaying themselves on their own terms. This recent order is a celestial order akin to that of the

Virgin Mary whose mantle of heavenly grace now begins to encompass Brigid, even in the "place" of her cult center. Here at St. Brigid's Well in Kildare we find a new vitality, but a vitality emanating from the Queen of Heaven manifest through Ireland's own Mary of the Gaels. Yet the water continues to flow ceaselessly through the stone paps.

A more conventional sign of atrophy is to be found at St. Brigid's Well in Cliffony, County Sligo. This well also had, until recently, borne evidence of the Celtic Brigid. The well is located in a cattle pasture. Local informants tell us that it has not been in use for twenty years. Beside the well was found in 1980 a standing stone, now in the form of a cross. On the head of the cross was clearly incised a swastika, symbol of the sun, and in this case the Otherworld sun, as the arms of the figure, as they rotated, dug into the earth much in the way the tines of a rototiller bury themselves to till the earth. On the edge of this stone, which was thirty-five inches high, were to be seen slashes that appear to be ogham, the early Celtic script. Obviously, the stone was of great antiquity. When we returned in 1987, the stone was gone. Local informants told us that there had been a pattern there as late as 1959. This date also appeared on a statue of St. Brigid still at the well and erected by a local family, the McHughs. Further, we were told that two hundred years ago there was a cattle fair held at the spot in conjunction with the pattern. These fairs were occasions for buying and selling, playing games, eating and drinking, and settling various feuds and quarrels that had arisen throughout the previous year. Such fairs were a direct descendant of the Celtic *oenach*, which were held at the critical times of the Celtic calendar and were part of the inauguration of the chief at the well site.

Another highly developed Brigid well is found in the small village of Liscannor, by the sea in County Clare. This site also retains much of the mother goddess symbolism in that the water from the well, located atop a small hill, flows through a hole into the interior of the hill where it is caught in a cistern of stone. Entry to the interior of the hill where the well is actually used is via a long cavelike passageway. This passageway is lined with various types of sanctions ranging from the crutches of healed cripples to petitions, pictures of the recently deceased, and holy pictures of saints including St. Brigid and her cow, as well as the more common medals and rosaries.

We were struck by the parallelism between the structure of this site dedicated to St. Brigid and New Grange, a pre-Celtic sacred mound also having

St. Brigid's Well, Liscannor, Co. Clare (45). Máire
MacNeill cites this as a Celtic site. Extremely well
cared for and active in 1994.

a long passage entry into a rounded chamber in keyhole form. It is the interior of such mountains and mounds that is the most powerful spot in cosmic religions and is the Otherworld and the dwelling place of the goddess in early Irish religion. Certainly the New Grange site had a great deal to do with fertility, the goddess, and the conception in her mound/womb of the new sun/son at the time of the death of the old sun/king on the winter solstice. It is on this date at 9:30 A.M. that the sun at its rising over the river Boyne, sacred to the goddess Boand, shines beneath the stone lintel of the passage entrance and directly down the passage and into the round chamber, in a miraculous feat of sacred engineering. It may be surmised, then, that it is at this moment that the new sun is conceived through the impregnation in the mound chamber of the old sun. In like manner, St. Brigid's Well at Liscannor may have been a place of rebirth, which occurred within its womb around the regenerating spring. As a site of Brigid, the ritual may have occurred on February 1, the feast of Brigid known as *imbolc,* which literally translated means "inbelly." The festival was associated with the lactation of ewes, that is, with their giving birth in the spring after their autumnal breeding. The structural correspondences between New Grange and St. Brigid's Well, Liscannor, are so striking that we seem safe in concluding that a Celtic fertility site existed at the well.

What we later discovered, however, is that the well is in fact a Celtic site but one celebrating the first fruits of autumn rather than the release of waters in springtime. Máire MacNeill describes St. Brigid's Well in Liscannor in great detail as an ancient Lughnasa site in conjunction with the nearby seaside resort of Lahinch. She also includes evidence that there was a pattern on St. Brigid's Day and wonders why the well is dedicated to St. Brigid if it is a Lughnasa site.[13]

Several factors can be considered in solving this interesting puzzle. First, the well was originally in a wooded grove, probably an oak grove. An inscription above the well in 1839 mentioned Brigid's association with the oak at Kildare (Cill-Dara, or Cell of the Oak). Second, MacNeill suggests that all the Lughnasa sites are burial sites of mythological women. Thus, the Liscannor site could combine the fertility of Brigid as "mythological woman" along with the harvest motifs of the August Lughnasa festival. Further, Lug is described by MacNeill as a god of the sun who could function as consort of the goddess at this site, now in the guise of Brigid.[14]

St. Brigid's Well, Liscannor, Co. Clare (45). The interior
location of the well is evidence of a goddess orientation.

The final factor we wish to note that has the most bearing on our interest in the transition from Brigid to Mary is that the pattern day has now shifted from the last Sunday in July to August 15. In other words, it has progressed from a festival celebrating a pre-Christian harvest rite to a festival celebrating the Assumption of the Blessed Virgin Mary, but at the same time the site retains the ancient name of Brigid.

In addition, this well, like St. Brigid's of Kildare, has been recently tidied. When we visited last in the spring of 1987, all the sanctions that had accumulated over the years had been removed. This recent phenomenon of ordering well sites by removing decaying or "unsightly" sanctions is antithetical to Irish tradition and sentiment. In fact, such tidying up seems to represent the celestial symbolism of order, emptiness, light, and vastness associated with pastoral nomadic and urban industrial cultures and with Protestantism. The Irish, having been involved in plant cultivation and the sea, are more attuned to the principle of decay through which new birth arises than with the creation through ordering so characteristic of industrial, nomadic, and hunting cultures.

Comparison of even contemporary Irish Catholic cemeteries with those in the industrialized United States or any Protestant-dominated nation gives witness to this. For the Irish, the cemetery appears to be a place of re-creation similar to a compost pile. Through the principle of decomposition and fermentation so characteristic of Celtic creative power, the soul is reconstituted and is transformed to new life, whether this new life be conceived as a form of transmigration or of a rebirth in an otherworld such as heaven. Whereas Irish Catholic graveyards are usually unkempt, often having unmowed grass, broken stones, and even exposed bones, those in Protestant-dominated areas such as the United States are maintained rigorously with the guarantee of "perpetual care" widely advertised by those who sell plots. In fact, the very use of stones is disappearing in Protestant graveyards in the United States in favor of the notion of the "peace garden," which looks simply like an open, neatly mowed lawn.

When we apply this distinction of creative principles to the tidying of a well that was originally a Lughnasa site related to death and rebirth through plant symbolism, and whose pattern day has been changed from the Lughnasa date to the festival of the Christian Queen of Heaven, we must conclude that some new influences have taken place that are changing the meaning of the well and its power. St. Brigid's Well at Liscannor is undergoing a stage of atrophy regarding the Celtic symbolism of Lughnasa and the fertility symbolism of Brigid. However, the site is being revitalized through the overlaying of the symbolism of the Queen of Heaven onto the earlier structure that itself is still tacitly surviving and is even influential in the forms of the cave entrance to the well, the oak, and the statue of St. Brigid. Each influences the other.

One last example of the tidy ordering principle as evidence of transformation of meaning is appropriate. St. Brigid's Well at Killaire, Co. Westmeath (55), is particularly old, as seen by its proximity to the hill of Uisneach. Uisneach was one of the two major ancient Irish religious centers, the other being Tara (56), the well-known royal site in Meath. Although Uisneach is not so prominent in the popular consciousness, it appears to have shared equal prestige with Tara. In a sense Uisneach was the "dark twin" of Tara as it represented the "primeval unity, the principle in which all oppositions are resolved."[15] Tara, on the other hand, symbolized the royal principle, the ordered cosmos. Within the society of ancient Ireland, Uisneach was represented by the druids and was emblematic of the queen, while Tara was represented by the nobles and was emblematic of the king. Still another suggestion is that Tara was concerned with the surface world while Uisneach was concerned with the Otherworld.

There are several references to a well at Uisneach, which itself was considered to be the navel of Ireland and the source of the twelve chief rivers of Ireland. The actual well, as center, had been lost, and there is a tale that tells how it was found by Oisín, son of Finn mac Cumaill. He went on a search for water for a feast. So as not to be followed while he looked for the hidden well, he walked backwards and in this manner found the "white-rimmed" well of Uisneach.[16] It is still not clear where that well is located, although we did find a double well, one flowing into the other, on our expedition there in 1981. There were no markings on the well nor any evidence of present-day use.

There is, however, a well dedicated to St. Brigid not more than a mile from the hill of Uisneach, located just one hundred yards from an establishment called the Uisneach Inn. Across the road from the inn is a stone clearly marked as the inauguration stone of the kings of Uisneach. The well is still active and includes several St. Brigid crosses as well as the remains of an oratory of St. Brigid.

An interesting bit of history surrounds the well and attests to its Celtic roots. Our informant, a local historian named Peter Ward, told us that the well was originally sacred to St. Aedh, which is anglicized to St. Hugh. St. Aedh's full name is St. Aedh mac Breac, and herein lies his relationship to Brigid and St. Brigid. This name carries with it two roots of meaning, Aedh and Breac. The former is the ancient Irish and Celtic name for the sun god and the Lord of the Otherworld, who was also husband of the Great Goddess, the land.[17] The second name, Breac, is a tribal name that generates from the originator of the tribe and relates to the goddess Brigit or Briget. Ordinarily the Irish word *breac* is translated as "speckled"; however, Hubert Butler in his controversial book *Ten Thousand Saints* suggests in a compelling way that this word, as used in tribal names, relates to a tribe that originated in Thrace and consequently migrated east to Asia and west through Gaul and into Ireland. Butler's conclusion might make sense when we see at St. Brigid's Well in Westmeath a linkage of both St. Aedh mac Breac and St. Bridget. In fact, Butler states that "it is curious that both in Wigtown and Westmeath it is not he [St. Aedh] but Brigit who is culted in the church [founded by him]."[18]

Looking a bit deeper into this conjunction, we find that the Celtic god Aedh was also the All Father of humankind, or Eochaid Ollathair, a name also attributed to the primal Irish god, the Dagda.[19] Further, we know that the Dagda was the father of the Great Goddess and Mother Brigid. Still further, O'Rahilly tells us that St. Aedh had several of the aspects of this ancient god of the sun attributed to him. He flew through the air in his chariot, he traveled in a chariot with a single wheel, and he warded off a deluge of rain from a cornfield.[20] Finally, Peter Ward, our local source, told us that St. Aedh caused the well to come forth, much in the manner of St. Bernadette of Lourdes, by scratching in the earth until the well flowed forth in order to find water for his mother so she would not have to go so far to gather it.

The well was renovated in 1979 by several local men, Peter Ward, Jim Malloy, Hugh Farrell, and Steven Daily. The renovation was part of a larger effort to tidy up the village area "for the Pride of Killaire" and as a means of highlighting the village's history. The fact that the well is a part of this historical preservation effort places it in the category of a quasi-exhibit, and such a status lays the well open to its removal from serious usage and integration in the daily and seasonal spiritual life of the community. It is not clear that this has in fact taken place at St. Brigid's Well in Killaire, but such historicization can often begin this type of atrophy. In such cases the wells are taken out of the sphere of the sacred and placed into that of the secular. It is a matter of removing the well from the mythological realm to the realm of history.

The old colloquialism "The more things change, the more they stay the same" seems to capture the particular process of development we have found in the holy wells of Ireland. The two factors that are part of this process of "development"—change and changelessness—exist at the same time yet are normally contradictory. They are present in varying ratios at differing points throughout the process.

This unique relationship of opposites is contained in the particular quality of syncretism present at these holy wells to this day. What we have discovered is that the past is present in the changes that seem to eclipse it. This manifests itself in the overt and covert influences of Celtic symbols and rituals that are still active at the wells despite the movement from orectic to normative, from loric to sacred. This coincidence is true despite the shift in emphasis at the wells from local to universal saints, from Brigid to Mary.

Finally, we have also seen power and influence moving in the other direction, that is, from the new to the old. Thus, the influence of the new Marian emphasis in its universalizing qualities is being felt at those wells that are still active and that still possess St. Brigid as their sacred figure. This strange and interesting process gives new life to the aphorism about change and perhaps helps us better to understand the symbolic nature of the Celtic spiral.

6

Mary as the Lady at the Well
in Modern Ireland

IN CONTRAST TO the degenerative situation surrounding St. Brigid wells, wells dedicated to the Virgin Mary seem to be growing. Several new sites sacred to the Madonna have established themselves very recently, one of them involving the birth of a new holy well. In counterbalance to the increasing predominance of Mary over Brigid in terms of quantity and activity, we also find that Brigid's power has an influence upon the quality of the manifestation at these Marian sites. Thus, what appears to be emerging is a form of syncretism in which the loric, in the figure of Brigid, presents itself in a quiet or tacit manner, while the sacred, in the figure of Mary, plays a predominant role in terms of the overt symbols that are present at the well. Thus, it is not simply a matter of Mary taking over Brigid wells but rather a change in the relationship of Brigid and Mary, the loric and the sacred. Through this change a syncretism has occurred between the two figures at the well. What results from this syncretism between the two figures is a change in the symbolic meaning of the holy well.

While keeping in mind what appears to be the syncretistic nature of the holy well in contemporary Ireland, we should like to focus now on several traditional "lady wells," but with an eye to the influence of Brigid and the loric upon the universal nature of the Christian saint rather than the influence of Mary on Brigid. Our examination of each well takes note of those features that tie it to its earlier roots in Brigid, the loric, and the earth. Such evidence as healings of the body, and especially the eyes, would link the well with

Brigid. Other lore, such as the fact that the well water percolates or that there is a magical trout living in the well, also would indicate early associations with Celtic and often Brigantine roots.

One of the most active lady wells we encountered in our fieldwork is located just outside the town of Millstreet in County Cork (57). We visited this well on Palm Sunday, 1987, and found a steady stream of pilgrims coming and going. Although the well has a name without relation to Christianity, simply Tobrid Well, it has been Christianized and highly developed at the expense of the natural setting. The well itself is a large and shallow kidney-shaped pool. It is a very strong and pure spring. Around the perimeter of the pool is laid a huge rosary with beads the size of bowling balls. The cross at the end of the rosary is situated at the tip of the pool just below a small footbridge over the pool. At this point the water in the huge spring can be seen to percolate. Approximately thirty feet from the pool a grotto has been constructed from natural materials, in which is situated a statue of Our Lady of Lourdes. Several old canes and crutches stand beside the statue, evidence of past healings. A rail around the grotto is used by pilgrims to pray upon before the Blessed Virgin. Just to the right of the grotto is a small blue altar sheltered by a shedlike canopy surmounted by a cross. In front of the complex is a large parking lot beside which is a modern toilet facility, indicating that the well is frequently used by many people. The entire site is located in a flat area and is akin to the umbilicus type of well.

In addition to its obvious Marian symbology, there are several indications of Celtic usage of the well that can be linked to Brigid. Regardless of whether we have direct evidence of a Brigantine connection, the influence of the Celtic aspects of the well are identified with the power of the loric, and thus indirectly and intentionally with Brigid.

We have already mentioned that the water percolates. This phenomenon was also found in the mythic Well of Segais and was identified in the myth with *na bolcca immaiss*, or bubbles of mystic inspiration, in other words, wisdom. Also, Brigid was the goddess most associated with wisdom and poetry. Another loric aspect of the well is that it is the home of a magical golden trout, also associated in Celtic Irish myth with wisdom in the form of the salmon and continued as loric custom to the present. Today, however, the sighting of a trout or salmon is often an omen of healing of the body. It is well known that both St. Brigit and the goddess Brigid were great healers.

St. Brigit is said to have healed various maladies including leprosy, muteness, and paralysis. One of the most interesting ways she healed was by the use of water. St. Brigit on one occasion blessed the water and placed it upon the afflicted area for healing. On another occasion she first changed the water into milk and used it to heal the affliction. In still another instance she healed with water from a ford in which she had slipped and cut her head. Her blood mixed with the water, and this was used to heal. She also healed with apples, the magical fruit of the Otherworld.[1] As the presence of crutches and canes about the statue of Mary substantiated, we were told that many healings have occurred at Tobrid Well over the past thirty years as a result of prayer to the Virgin and the drinking of water from the well.

The Marian associations are numerous and seem to have taken up the original loric power and made use of it. Thus, it is not simply the superimposed Lady of Lourdes that does the healing but the water from the well in conjunction with the Virgin.

Another highly developed Marian well is located near the town of Ballyheige in County Kerry (58). When we use the term "highly developed," we refer to well sites in which the natural setting has been reordered or overlaid by human construction. This is typical of many modern Marian wells, and Ballyheige is an excellent example. In effect, the entire site has been arranged into a garden that depicts, through a process of walking from plot to plot, the entire Christian salvation history from the Garden of Eden to the crucifixion of Christ. The garden is neatly laid out and well cared for. It is on the order of an English formal garden. The well is situated at the end of the process that coincides with the entrance to the site. There is also a shed facing the well, nicely appointed, in which pilgrims can rest and contemplate the well and the large statue of the Virgin Mary that looks down upon it. Also found in another shed are the stations of the cross. The site is near a road on fairly level land and is well marked. The round or pattern consists of all fifteen decades of the rosary recited while passing along the path that leads through the salvation history. One finishes at the well and drinks therefrom, setting forth one's petition to the Virgin Mary. The pattern day falls on September 8, the birthday of the Blessed Virgin Mary; and the instructions for the walking of the rosary path indicate that the round ends at the birth of Mary. In other words, from the perspective of this ritual, the salvation history culminates with the nativity of the Mother of God.

Despite the high level of Marian sanctions, iconography, and ritual, there remains a quiet influence of Celtic symbolism that is built into the traditions of the well and coexists with the Christian material without apparent contradiction. For example, there is a legend of a sacred trout that lives in the well. Further, the trout is linked to another symbol of Celtic power, the percolation of the water of the well. It is said by local pilgrims that if the water of the well percolates, the trout is present. We know from Irish mythology that both these phenomena are symbolic of the watery wisdom possessed by the goddess and that Brigit herself was giver and possessor of this wisdom.

The water of the well is also known for its curative powers. Although these cures may now be attributed to Mary's presence at the well, it is likely that cures were attained before the coming of Mary to the well and were due to the power of the water itself. We were told during our expedition there in 1980 that the well cures various diseases, and several recent and specific cures were reported to us. We were told that there was a recent cure of severe arthritis. Another report concerned the complete cure of a victim of cancer who is still living in the nearby town of Tarbert. Finally, we must note that the water is taken internally for a cure in accordance with the Celtic custom, rather than being applied externally as in the Christian tradition. It is also taken to homes where it is used in the manner of holy water in the Christian custom; that is, it is sprinkled upon the object to be blessed.

One final example should suffice to demonstrate the influence of Brigid and the loric on the wells of the Virgin Mary. Tobernault, located by Lough Gill and just outside the city of Sligo, is perhaps one of the most active wells in Ireland today. It is likely that activity at the well has not stopped completely since earliest times. MacNeill indicates that the well was a site at which the Lughnasa festival, one of the quaternary festivals of the Celtic year, was celebrated. In fact, the chief pattern at the well today is held on Garland (or Garlic) Sunday, the last Sunday of July, which is within the octave of the Lughnasa festival, which falls on August 1.[2] This fact alone attests to the ancient nature of the well and its grounding in the loric, still present in the dating of the major pattern day.

However, there are other aspects of the well that amplify its Celtic usage. The name itself makes no reference to any Christian phenomena. It refers either to a part of the body, a joint, the head, or to the place in which the well is situated, perhaps a cliff or ravine. All of these translations carry with them significance within the Celtic tradition. The reference to the head is supported by the curative powers of the well that were at one time directed primarily to the cure of head pains. We were told that there is a special stone in the wall of the well that is used for the curing of headaches. One wades into the well and places one's head upon the stone.

There are other signs of Celtic usage. The location itself is reminiscent of early sacred groves. The well is located in a grove, and its *bile,* or sacred tree, is an oak, sacred to the druids. Still another indication of the early nature of the site is the fact that its healing powers are most effective at night, the time of fecundity and new beginnings in Celtic tradition. There is also a sacred trout in the well and tales about it being caught by a traveler. The traveler tried to cook the fish, and it leaped out of the frying pan and back into the well. Finally, within the collection of sanctions at the well were clooties, pieces of ribbon, cloth, and paper tied to a sacred tree by the statue of St. Anne, mother of St. Mary. There is also a sacred stone by the well, which is said to have embedded in it the fingerprints of St. Patrick. The stone is now called a "wishing bed" and is used to cure ailments of the back and to grant wishes of the pilgrims who place their hand upon the fingerprints of Patrick. It is most likely that this stone with its extraordinary configuration filled out the ancient complex of rock, tree, and water that constituted the microcosmic components of the Celtic sacred spring.

In its present state the well is overtly dominated by symbols from the Christian tradition, especially that of Marian devotion. A steep wooded hill rising directly behind the well is included within the well's precincts. Halfway up this hill on the right is located a Lourdes grotto built into the rock face of the hill. Votive candles are in active use, as well as flowers and a sacred tree in which are found clooties, rosaries, and other sanctions. On the left and at about the same level is a shrine of the Crucifixion. Beneath a life-size cross upon which Christ hangs are standing figures of the Blessed Virgin, Mary Magdalene, and John the Beloved Apostle. Around the well itself within the level wooded area that lies before it runs a path for ritual rounds. The notion of a round or circumambulation of a sacred spring is certainly of Celtic origin, but on the path now are located the fourteen stations of the cross. In addition, there is a shrine to St. Anne, located across the path from station six. Finally, within the well itself and near the stone to be touched for cure of head pains is located a plaque upon which is engraved "O Mary, conceived without sin, pray for us who have recourse to Thee." The entire complex presents us with a moving and beautiful synthesis of Celtic and Christian power, of loric and sacred, of Brigid and Mary.

When we visited Tobernault in April 1987, we were alone at the site surrounded by the peace and tranquillity that it manifests. A lone workman arrived in a lorry and got out to kneel before the brook that runs out of the well and wash his eyes. We observed quietly, a feeling of awe welling up within us. At length, he approached and engaged us in conversation. He asked us the question we wanted to hear most. Did we want to know anything about the well? In the course of the conversation we asked him about a small pin he was wearing on his jacket. Behind the pin, which was in the image of a golden rose, lay a story that involved Tobernault and that pointed beyond this well to the final phase of our study.

Our new acquaintance was a cement worker, Pádraic Scanlon, and some years ago a reinforcement rod had run into his eye.[3] He was in danger of losing the eye and was in a hospital in Dublin awaiting an operation that all hoped would save it. Shortly before his scheduled operation, a friend from Sligo visited. He asked Pádraic if he could apply some water from Tobernault to the eye, just as a last resort. Pádraic, in his vulnerable state, consented. Several days later, but still before the scheduled operation, the eye was sufficiently healed to delay the operation. Still later, the eye was declared completely well. At that moment Pádraic made a promise to the Virgin Mary that he would visit Tobernault every day, wash his eyes in the sacred waters, and pray to her in thanksgiving.

Just as we were about to leave this sacred place to continue our fieldwork in Donegal, Pádraic, almost as a footnote, told us that the Virgin Mary actually had appeared to some local schoolgirls not far away near a small village called The Culleens. The fact of such an apparition was not directly connected to our work on holy wells, but it was certainly of general interest to the historian of religion. While we were in the wildness of North Donegal, we began to think that perhaps there was a connection between the appearances of the Virgin Mary in Ireland and the ancient lady at the well. Could the lady be appearing now in modern Christian form with a message not for the kings of ancient Ireland but for the entire world, a message that is grounded in the power of place, the well? Could these modern postindustrial apparitions be a survival of earlier myth and ritual modes appearing at a different point in history and thus presenting a universalized message? Could this phenomenon be part of a natural dynamic of power that moves from loric to sacred, from orectic to normative?

As time went on, these thoughts became rather compelling, and we decided to visit the site at The Culleens (59). Here it was said that the Virgin Mary had appeared in the sky to several teenage girls in September 1986. What we were particularly interested in determining was if water in any form was connected with the appearances of our Lady. This was important, because if water did play a significant part in the apparitions, it was likely that some form of syncretism had occurred between early Celtic spring and river goddesses (e.g., Brigit) and the modern Virgin Mary. We arrived at this conclusion based on a provocative suggestion made by Anne Ross. She writes: "It may not be too far from the truth to suggest that the goddesses in whom fertility and maternity played a predominant part were connected with horses, but not of course exclusively. In the same way it could be suggested that the goddesses associated with rivers and springs had especial connections with cows, and the war goddesses with carrion birds."[4] Thus Brigid would be a model spring goddess, associated with fertility and the power of earth and the water of life that flows therefrom. If Mary also carries on this tradition, she becomes a modern universalized version of an ancient and loric symbol of the lady of the well.

When we headed south from Donegal, we stopped at the site of the apparition at The Culleens. At this point we recalled hearing of statues of the Virgin Mary that were seen to move at several sites in Ireland recently. Could this phenomenon also be linked to the apparitions and thus point back to the ancient spring goddess? The year in which many of these phenomena began occurring was 1985. The first reported instance occurred in a church in the small village of Asdee, County Kerry. There a seven-year-old girl saw two statues in the church move. The first was a statue of Jesus with his heart exposed. The statue beckoned to the little girl. The second statue was of the Virgin Mary, whose eyes moved. It is interesting that this event concerning the "sacred heart of Jesus" occurred on February 14, 1985, St. Valentine's Day.

In March of the same year another group of children claimed to have seen a statue of Jesus of the sacred heart move in the church of St. Patrick located in Ballydesmond, County Cork. The following July two adult women reported seeing a statue of the Virgin Mary move. This statue was outdoors and was a model of the apparition at Lourdes. The statue is located near the top of a small hill. At the foot of the hill and looking up at the Virgin is a statue of St. Bernadette; there is a stream running by St. Bernadette. This event is the first example focused exclusively on the Virgin Mary. It is also the first to occur outdoors in a natural setting, a "place," and the first to involve a natural water formation, the small stream. The site is located near the town of Ballinspittle in County Cork. Following this event, accounts of miraculous appearances and moving statues increased, and by late September 1985 over thirty such accounts had been reported.[5]

We visited three of these sites: The Culleens, Ballinspittle (60), and Mount Melleray (61). We had documented another one, a Lourdes type of grotto called Gortaneadin Grotto, located on the Dunmanway side of Inchigeela in County Cork (62), in March 1985. It was in August of that year that the alleged apparition took place. All four of these sites had some connection with water. Three of them concerned apparitions and one a moving statue. Two of the apparitions are said to have given messages and spoken to the seers. Three of the four sites are models of the apparition at Lourdes where Bernadette Soubirous was told by the "Lady" to dig in the earth for a spring. When she did so, a spring appeared and remains flowing today. The water is said to have considerable curative power.

Let us begin our review of these sites with the one we have not visited since the apparition occurred there in August 1985, Inchigeela. We stopped at this site on our way to a well-known holy well, St. Finbar's Well (63) and hermitage. We were attracted by the beautiful brook that rushes down the hillside between the statue of our Lady and Bernadette. Had there not been water in conjunction with the shrine, we would have passed it by. Our inquiries revealed that indeed the water was considered to be special, if not sacred, as it was drunk ritually by those visiting the shrine. There was a date on the cement railing in front of the site reading 1944. It is difficult to tell if the site was active before the building of the shrine due to the power of the waters or not. Our informant told us that there were no reported cures that she knew of. We spoke to only one informant and took no pictures.

We were at the shrine at Inchigeela on March 22, 1985; and on the following August 5 two young girls, Rosemary O'Sullivan and Marie Vaughan, claimed to have seen an appearance of the Blessed Virgin there. What they allegedly saw was not a statue that moved as reported at Ballinspittle but a separate image, not attached to the earth, that seemed to be alive. These two girls, along with several others, reported that the apparition spoke to them and gave them several messages. Although we have no direct evidence, it is very likely that the water took on a more vital power after this event and was probably connected in people's minds with the Virgin's appearance.

The Culleens is a small village in County Sligo situated between the Sliabh Damh, or Ox Mountains, and Killala Bay. It was in a small section of this locality called Carns that the following event took place; thus, this apparition is called Our Lady of Carns. This is the only site we visited where there had not been an already existing shrine. In fact, the apparition occurred in a boggy pasture in a virtually uninhabited area. The apparition took the form of a light in the sky in which the Virgin appeared to four young schoolgirls. She gave no messages. There is nothing striking about the place other than the fact that it is a bog, a watery piece of land, and that bogs were often, like wells, places of votive deposits. In other words, like wells, they provided access to the Otherworld goddess beneath the earth's surface by means of their absorbing and porous nature. They were thus considered, in many instances within Celtic tradition, to be sacred space, a part of the goddess, and, as at the well, offerings were thrown into the site. Thus, the site at The Culleens participates as a variant in the complex of rock, tree, and water that we have noted in connection with recent reported apparitions in Ireland.[6]

The importance of the power of "place" is enhanced in this apparition because of the lack of any previously placed religious artifacts synthesized by human hands. We must assume that the action of the sacred is never arbitrary or meaningless, and thus the Virgin Mary chose to appear at this particular place with only natural features precisely because of those natural features, chief of which is the boggy ground above which she is said to have appeared. We can go on to infer that natural features must play a symbolic role in the sites where there were synthesized religious images as well. This is not to say that the religious images are now rendered meaningless, but that there appears a complex of symbols, some natural, some synthetic, or manmade, that complement one another to form a whole meaning.[7]

The site near Ballinspittle, a small village in County Cork, not far from the city of Cork, is a shrine site built in 1954 to commemorate the centenary of the Immaculate Conception. There are two statues, one of Our Lady of the Immaculate Conception and one of St. Bernadette. Thus, like Inchigeela, the site imitates Lourdes where the miraculous healing spring was unearthed by Bernadette at the command of the Virgin Mary. This is also a hillside site and has water in the form of a small stream flowing at the bottom of the hill. It is interesting to note that when we visited the site on Passion Sunday of 1987, we found that the stream had been diverted in order to make room for more seating. Nonetheless, the site retains the primary structure of the well site with its rock, tree, and water.

The Ballinspittle site was one of the moving statue phenomena rather than an apparition, but we chose to include it because of the presence of the Lady at a natural water formation. It is also important in that it is one of the Lourdes imitations where a sacred spring was established by the Lady through her directives to Bernadette.

We now turn to the final example, the shrine at Mount Melleray, not far from the Cistercian monastery of the same name. It is located about six miles from the small town of Cappoquin in County Waterford. This shrine is yet another example of the Lourdes imitation and was placed there by Father Celestine of the monastery in 1982. Once again, the "place" seems to be of primary importance in the establishment and maintenance of power. This is true for two reasons: the Virgin always appears at or near the same place, and the structure of the place seems constant throughout the sites of the various apparitions and moving statue occurrences with its incorporation of a natural setting involving water and often a tree and stone. We find just such a site at Mount Melleray.

The geography of the site is very pronounced in its relation to water and the feminine. To begin with, the configuration of the land at the site is that of a small, steep valley that is wooded. Running along the base of one of the hills of this miniature valley is a small brook that empties into the river Glenshelane. This river flows through the valley and is bridged just at the place of the grotto. The hillside from which the brook flows is wooded and has many scrub plants and grasses growing on it. On this hill the statue of the Immaculate Conception was placed in 1982, and at its base, near the brook, was placed a statue of Bernadette looking up at our Lady. One descends to the base of the hill from the level of the bridge, now on a newly built stairway. The entire site is saturated with fertility, and if Ireland were imaged as a goddess as in Celtic myth, the site would resemble the place of fertility of greatest importance, her *yoni*.[8] It clearly retains the feeling and structure of the pre-Christian sacred grove with its sacred spring, tree, and stone.

In fact, there is an ancient stone cross that is being repaired at the top of the descent into the valley. Further, several trees by the brook are decorated with candles and sacred pictures, as well as clooties. The brook has been made into a pool and stoned inside, just at the foot of the hill. Thus we have the image of the sacred spring. Taken as a whole, the site follows the pattern of the holy well with its rock, tree, and water symbolism.

Some of the events and messages that were given at Mount Melleray provide information that establishes a new holy well and demonstrates the syncretic nature of the Marian phenomena, even in recent times. The events at Mount Melleray grotto began on Friday, August 16, 1985, and the visions and messages lasted until the following Saturday, August 24. One of the distinguishing characteristics of the events at Mount Melleray, as recounted by the witnesses, is that the image of the Virgin Mary detached itself from the statue and walked down the hill. She also talked to several people, both children and adults. Thus we are dealing with an apparition rather than simply a moving statue, although many have reported seeing the statue move without seeing a detached image.

It was on Sunday, August 18, after two days of seeing the moving statue, that the apparition first appeared, according to the testimony of a local farmer, Michael O'Donnell, who said: "Suddenly the whole background of the statue changed with steps towards the front. Our Lady took the form of a real woman and began walking down the steps." On the next day, Monday, August 19, the first of the reported messages from our Lady concerning the power of the place was given. For our purposes this is the most important and decisive confirmation of the loric element of power that continues to reside within the contemporary lady at the well and at the site that she empowers. Barry Buckley and his cousin Tom Cliffe, two of the three primary visionaries, were at the grotto and reported seeing our Lady step out of the statue and the stairs appear that led from the place of the statue on the hillside down to the water's edge. They then reported seeing her walk down the steps, which were of brown clay with multicolored roses, some very large, at both sides of the steps. At the bottom of the steps she turned to her left a few paces to the water's edge in front of the boys. "Then Our Lady said to the boys: 'My message is peace and prayer. Tell the people that the water is blessed.'"[9]

This reported message establishes the power of the place as manifested through the water, and it essentially represents the emergence of a new holy well over which the Virgin presides, as the lady at the well. But we also have recent evidence of the healing power of this site even before the apparitions of the Virgin Mary there in August 1985. On January 19, 1985, it was reported that a beautiful Bible was found wrapped in a plastic bag and placed on a seat in the grotto. On the inside cover was the following inscription: "I donate this Bible to this shrine where I found some Miraculous cures. It will be remembered in my prayers." Dr. William Deevy continues, "So the Grotto has been a holy place for some time, possibly since the monks had their first home on the mountain just across the river, but certainly since Fr. Celestine in his foresight had the statue of Our Lady erected there in 1982."[10] It may also be possible that the place had revealed its healing power long before the coming of the monks.

There is another aspect of the Melleray apparition that grounds it in the loric. Loric power was manifest in the notion, present in Celtic Ireland, of the *tuath*, which originally was the name for a people but came also to mean a geographical complex that constituted the place of habitation of the clan unit. Thus, the people were thought of as being born from the place, which was alive and envisioned as a goddess. More precisely, the people, or their representative, the chief, were married to the place/goddess. The *tuath* was the symbol of the conjunction of the people and goddess and evidence of the special relationship of a particular people to a particular place/goddess. This same ancient relationship of a special people devoted to a place/goddess is established by the reported messages of our Lady at Melleray, who is the lady of the well or the source and functions as the *deus loci*.

It was on Tuesday, August 20, 1985, that the Virgin Mary first renewed this ancient bond, initially established by Brigid as mother goddess of Ireland and later by her Christian counterpart, St. Bridget, "Mary of the Gael." On that evening, after asking for several rosaries, the Virgin Mary was reported to have said to the boys: "I love the Irish people. I am praying with the people to God, to forgive the Irish people. I want the Irish people to spread my message to the world." The following evening, Wednesday, August 21, the Virgin Mary continued her calling to the people of Ireland. She is reported by the boys to have said: "God is pleased with Ireland. Ireland will be saved. I want the people of Ireland to convey my message to the world."[11] It is also significant that during the recitation of the rosary on the first of these two evenings, the boys noticed that the apparition of the Virgin Mary was praying along with them in the Irish language, again symbolic of her connection to place. Everybody else, including the visionaries, was praying in English.

While these reported messages of the Virgin reestablish the ancient bond of the people with the goddess of the place, they also point beyond Ireland and Mount Melleray to the world. In other words, they initiate a process of universalization, the same process we see in the movement from Brigid to St. Bridget to Mary. Within this process the Irish have been called to establish her message not only in the place, in Ireland, but throughout the world. This emphasis on universalizing power and world is found in several other reported messages at Melleray, messages that establish the sacred through the loric: "The world must improve. The world has ten years to improve. It must improve ten times," and "The world must behave. I want the world to believe me. I want the world to get my message. I want all of ye to tell the world. Ye have ways of telling the world. My message is peace and prayer and no more fighting in the world."[12]

Thus the universal is possible through the particular, the sacred through the loric. They dwell together, reflecting upon and enhancing one another in the process of the achievement of wholeness or "salvation." What emerges graphically is a spirallike pattern in which the opposites, loric and sacred, coexist in a dialectical relationship; but at the same time they are moving "ahead" from particular to universal, from loric to sacred, from Ireland to the world.

The identification of this spirallike movement in the symbolic history of the holy wells of Ireland brings us to the end of our study. We have tried to emphasize the importance of the very existence and use of holy wells in Ireland today, for sacred springs are among the most ancient of religious phenomena that have a continuity of religious usage from prehistoric times to the present. We have tried to point out this continuity of early Irish Celtic myth with current folklore and Christian ritual practices through descriptions gleaned from our own fieldwork and from the work of others. We have also attempted to identify in this history of holy wells a syncretism of Celtic and Christian symbolism and the reflection of this syncretism in two forms of power, the loric and the sacred. We paid special attention to the bridge symbols that made possible this unique syncretism at the wells. Finally, we hope that we have conveyed to the reader our love for these wells and for the Irish people, who from the most ancient times to the present worship there.

GLOSSARY

NOTES

BIBLIOGRAPHY

INDEX

Glossary

À soliel: in the direction of the sun, as in the king's circuit.

Axis mundi: pole of the world, center pole, the world axis.

Bachall Ísu: the staff or crozier purportedly given to St. Patrick by an angel of God and used by Patrick to perform extraordinary feats of transformation.

Bile: a sacred tree.

Booley stone: a special family stone used to activate a well for healing, or to "bring butter."

Bridget's cross: an ancient cross originally fashioned in the form of a right-handed swastika.

Butter stone: a special stone believed to hasten the coming of butter in the churn. Sometimes called a booley stone.

Clooties (or cloties): rags or threads left upon a tree, bush, or rock to absorb or take away a disease or difficulty, usually found in proximity to a holy well.

Deus loci: local or loric god, having a limited tribal jurisdiction or influence.

Egg stone: smooth egg-shaped stones believed to be petrified snake or dragon eggs congealed at the time of St. Patrick's expulsion of snakes (hags) from Ireland. These objects represent fertility and are often placed by women at holy wells for fertility, especially at the "vagina" wells found near the sea.

Fons et origo: the original source of water, life. The Well of Segais is an example of this form of spring.

Garlic Sunday: properly called Garland Sunday; a festival that Máire MacNeill connects with Lughnasa, the end of waiting for new crops, when the new potatoes may be eaten.

Geis: a taboo or prohibition concerning the behavior of a particular king in early Irish social structure.

Lia Fáil: a stone now said to be at Tara, which determined the true king.

Magna mater: great mother (goddess).

Na bolcca immaiss: bubbles of wisdom contained in sacred springs.

Ogham: the early Irish script found mainly on boundary stones usually defining tribal or local territory by ancestry.

Patterns, or "patrons": set ways of traveling around or near sacred sites, particularly wells or saints' "beds," interspersed with prayers that are most efficacious on certain days of the week or year or at a specific hour of a particular day and sometimes performed in kneeling position.

Poitín: a high-proof potato liquor.

Sain: saining was a ritual purification that Patrick performed at many wells with his staff.

Sanctions: the many offerings found at the holy wells.

Senex: an archetype of the old man.

Síd: underground caves or circles under mounds to which the early mythological settlers of Ireland retreated.

Súil: Irish word for "eyes."

Tuath: a unit of people and their land that had common loric or tribal social patterns under the rule of a clan chieftain/king.

Notes

Introduction

1. O.S. Leitrim 33, N 10, Ordinance Survey Letters, Ordinance Survey Office, Phoenix Park, Dublin.

2. Many wells seeking vengeance are recorded in our files. See also MacNeill, *The Festival of Lughnasa*, appendix 2, no. 185, for a description of Peakaun's Well, and p. 626 for further examples. The material on St. John's Well is found in our file no. 14 and was given by a local informant.

3. Balla, Co. Mayo, was also the site of a festival called "O Baal" in which "not less than three hundred sheep" were consumed, according to Dr. J. M'Parlan, in Statistical Survey of Mayo, 1801, p. 130, as quoted by MacNeill, *The Festival of Lughnasa*, p. 59.

4. See Logan, *The Holy Wells of Ireland*, for general descriptions of Irish holy wells with an eye toward their healing powers within a Christian context.

5. See Brenneman, *Spirals*, chaps. 3 and 4, for a thorough discussion of myth and ritual as historical forms.

6. See Eliade, *Cosmos and History*.

7. See Eliade, *Patterns in Comparative Religion*, chaps. 4–8, for a discussion of the symbolic connections of plant, water, moon, and woman. See also Bleakley, *The Fruits of the Moon Tree*, p. 240ff., for a perceptive interpretation of menstruation and menstrual blood.

8. See Long, *Alpha*, p. 224ff., for an account of this myth. Jensen, *Myth and Cult among Primitive Peoples*, pp. 107–20, also presents an interesting interpretation of this myth.

1. The Nature of the Sacred Spring

1. Ross, *Pagan Celtic Britain*, pp. 21, 38.

2. The Well of Segais is described as an Otherworld well with hazel trees and salmon in Rees and Rees, *Celtic Heritage*, pp. 161, 349.

3. Montague, *Faber Book of Irish Verse*, p. 45.

4. Ibid., p. 90.

5. Ibid., p. 42.

6. Ross, *Pagan Celtic Britain*, p. 6.

7. Eliade, *Patterns in Comparative Religion*, pp. 200–201.

8. Ross, *Pagan Celtic Britain*, p. 21.

9. See Markale, *Celtic Civilization*, p. 29, for an exposition of the "submerged town" motif in Irish Celtic myths of origin.

10. Balor's Raid may be found in O'Donovan, *The Annals of the Kingdom of Ireland by the Four Masters from the Earliest Period to the Year 1616*, pp. 18–23.

11. Ó hAodha, *Bethu Brigte*, p. 23.

12. Montague, *Faber Book of Irish Verse*, p. 49.

2. Myth and Ritual at Celtic Irish Springs

1. See Chadwick, *The Celts*, chap. 1, for a further discussion of the agricultural roots of Celtic culture.

2. Markale, *Celtic Civilization*, chap. 1, gives an in-depth study of this cosmogonic theme throughout Celtic culture.

3. This myth is found in the *Leabhar Gabhála Erin*, translated by d'Arbois de Jubainville as *The Irish Mythological Cycle*.

4. Gwynn, *The Metrical Dindshenchas*.

5. Mac Cana, *Celtic Mythology*, p. 120.

6. Dillon and Chadwick in *Celtic Realms* state, "The word [tuath] means 'tribe', 'people', and is used also for the territory they inhabit" (p. 86).

7. See Brenneman, "Serpents, Cows, and Ladies," for a thorough discussion of these factors.

8. See Brenneman, *Spirals*, p. 65ff., for an elaboration of the quality of myth.

9. The *Lia Fál* or *Lia Fáil* means in Irish "circle stone" or "stone fence." Fál also refers to a circlet worn on the wrist or arm. Occasionally fáil means "bright" or "light." In essence, the *Lia Fáil* refers to a stone of light that is circular and is the earthly counterpart of the King of the Heavens, the sun. See O'Rahilly, *Early Irish History and Mythology*, p. 521, n. 1, for a discussion of this etymology and its symbolic implications. The spear of Lug was brought by the Tuatha Dé Danann, the people of the goddess, to Ireland. Lug was a young, bright god of these people and possessor of this spear. Nuadu was a mythical Lord of the Otherworld and is often cited as first father of humankind (see O'Rahilly, *Early Irish History and Mythology*, p. 467ff.). He was also king of the Tuatha Dé Danann and commanded them in the famous battles of Mag Tured. The Dagda was also a Lord of the Otherworld and had an underground palace called Brugh na Bóinne.

10. See Gwynn, *The Metrical Dindshenchas* 3:286ff., for the complete myth and the reference to this well.

11. The cycles are the Mythological Cycle, whose events refer back to the biblical era; the Ulster or Red Branch Cycle, dating from about the Christian era; the Fianna Cycle, approximately the third century A.D.; and the Historical Cycle or Cycle of the Kings, referring to events occurring from the third century B.C. to the eighth century A.D.

12. A síd (pronounced *shee*) is a mound within which Otherworld gods and goddesses live and which offers access, through some orifice, between the worlds. This is the same mound that forms a central part of the holy well complex where chieftains were inaugurated.

13. These myths are summarized from the versions given by O'Rahilly, *Early Irish History and Mythology*, pp. 326–29.

14. The divine smith is another version of the Lord of the Otherworld, father to the son/challenger who seeks his kingship. See ibid., p. 60, for a discussion of this identity.

15. Rees and Rees, *Celtic Heritage*, pp. 73, 75.

16. See ibid., p. 298ff., for a summary of this tale.

17. Sjoestedt, *Gods and Heroes of the Celts*, pp. 35, 53.

18. See ibid., p. 52ff.

19. Ibid., p. 55.

20. Kinsella, *The Tain*, p. 250.

21. O'Rahilly is cited from Draak, "Some Aspects of Kingship in Pagan Ireland," in *The Sacral Kingship*, pp. 659–60.

22. See Joyce, *Social History of Ancient Ireland* 1:45.

23. See Bleakley, *The Fruits of the Moon Tree*, p. 105.

24. Joyce, *Social History of Ancient Ireland*, pp. 49–50.

25. Cormacán Éigeas, "A Poem on the Circuit of Ireland by Muircheartach MacNeill (919–943)," in O'Donovan, *Tracts Relating to Ireland*, p. 29.

26. Macalister, *Tara, a Pagan Sanctuary of Ancient Ireland*, pp. 28–29.

27. Ibid., p. 28.

28. O'Rahilly, *Early Irish History and Mythology*, p. 60.

29. Ibid., pp. 58, 60.

30. This quote is found in both Dumezil, *The Destiny of a King*, p. 88, and Mac Cana, *Celtic Mythology*, p. 120.

31. Joyce, *Social History of Ancient Ireland*, pp. 43–50.

32. Mac Cana, *Celtic Mythology*, p. 120.

33. Hutton, *The Pagan Religions of the Ancient British Isles*, p. 173.

34. Rees and Rees, *Celtic Heritage*, p. 52.

35. See T. G. E. Powell, *The Celts*, pp. 152–53; Sjoestedt, *Gods and Heroes of the Celts*, p. 69. Arabagian, in her article "Cattle Raiding and Bride Stealing," p. 135, states, "It appears, thus, that the bull, not the cow, is construed as *the* sacrificial animal . . . perhaps an embodiment of the dying/rising god."

36. See Ross, *Pagan Celtic Britain*, pp. 22–25.

37. See Powell, *The Celts*, pp. 148–51. We referred earlier in this chapter to the myth of Nial and the hag to illustrate the association of the well with wisdom and sovereignty (*flaith*). But that same myth also illustrates the theme here mentioned of transformation through sacrificial death. The sacrifice is to kiss the hag, to give one's life (eros) to her. When this sacrifice is made, she is reborn into a beautiful maiden.

3. Loric Power at the Wells

1. See Brenneman and Yarian, *The Seeing Eye*, chap. 8, and Walter L. Brenneman, Jr., "The Circle and the Cross: Loric and Sacred Space in the Holy Wells of Ireland," in Seaman and Mugerauer, *Dwelling Place and Environment*, pp. 137–59, for a thorough discussion of these two forms of power.

2. The Irish word *tuath* refers not only to a place or holding of land but also to the people who live thereon. Thus it has a double meaning that incorporates the people and the place of their habitation.

3. See Ross, *Pagan Celtic Britain*, pp. 61–127, for a thorough discussion of the Celtic cult of the head.

4. Foucault in his *The Order of Things*, p. 27, in a discussion of symbolic resemblances, mentions the association of the nut with the head and the brain and refers to a seventeenth-century source by O. Crollius titled *Traité des signatures*.

5. Bleakley, *The Fruits of the Moon Tree*, p. 105.

6. Lucas, "The Sacred Trees of Ireland," p. 42.

7. Bleakley, *The Fruits of the Moon Tree*, p. 100.

8. Ibid., p. 101 and n. 30, p. 286.

9. Information gathered from an interview in the field, April 1981.

10. Rees and Rees, *Celtic Heritage*, pp. 29–30.

11. Ross, *Pagan Celtic Britain*, p. 104.

12. Ibid., pp. 62, 151–52.

13. Logan, *The Holy Wells of Ireland*, p. 24.

14. Ibid., p. 23.

15. Ross, *Pagan Celtic Britain*, p. 345, refers to the fact that the Celts of Gaul revered the serpent's egg, presumably for its fertilizing power. This belief was recorded by Pliny. When the motif came to Ireland, the egg of the serpent turned to stone after Patrick's victory over the serpents/monsters on Croagh Patrick and in the Lughnasa festival where Patrick defeated the monster Crom Dubh. See MacNeill, *The Festival of Lughnasa*, pp. 409–17, for a detailed discussion of the myth of Crom Dubh.

16. Evans, *Irish Folk Ways*, p. 197.

17. Ibid., p. 95.

18. See Neumann, *The Great Mother*, pp. 39–47, for a discussion of the vessel-woman-body-world symbolism.

19. Ordinance Survey Letters, 2:235ff., Ordinance Survey Office, Phoenix Park, Dublin.

20. Logan, *The Holy Wells of Ireland*, p. 81.

4. The Coming of Patrick

1. It was the dating of Easter that was one of the main points that separated the Celtic Catholic and Roman Catholic churches at the Synod of Whitby in 664.

2. See Husserl, *The Idea of Phenomenology*, lecture 4, for a concise discussion of intentionality.

3. Hall, *Dictionary of Subjects and Symbols in Art*, p. 122.

4. Livingstone, *The Concise Oxford Dictionary of the Christian Church*, p. 194.

5. See Butler, *Ten Thousand Saints*, for a provocative discussion of the origin of saints' names.

6. Eliade, *Patterns in Comparative Religion*, p. 292.

7. Stokes, *The Tripartite Life of Patrick*.

8. See Hood, *St. Patrick and His Writings*, introduction pp. 6–7.

9. This prophecy is translated by James Carney in Montague, *Faber Book of Irish Verse*, p. 49. Montague places the piece under the heading of "Old Mythologies," and it is in this spirit that we use the text. Whether this text is Christian fabrication or authentic Celtic prophecy translated by Christians, its mythological intentionality remains the same.

10. Ibid., p. 48.

11. See Stokes, *The Tripartite Life of Patrick* 1:47, for a version of St. Patrick as shape-shifter.

12. Ibid., 2:445, gives an account of Patrick's refusal to take the staff of the hag. Dillon in *The Cycles of the Kings*, p. 40, discusses the horrible hag as an archetypal figure.

13. Other examples of the power of the *Bachall Ísu* may be found in Stokes, *The Tripartite Life of Patrick* 1:cii ff., where Crom Cruaich is destroyed and Patrick is seen slaying druids and marking out boundaries with the staff.

14. MacNeill, *The Festival of Lughnasa*, pp. 113–14.

15. Stokes, *The Tripartite Life of Patrick* 1:101.

16. Ibid., p. 103.

17. The complete tale of Queen Medb is found in Kinsella, *The Tain*, p. 250.

5. From Brigid to Mary

1. Lonegren, *Spiritual Dowsing*, p. 34. Primary water is not ground water resulting from rainfall but is rather the by-product of chemical reactions taking place under the earth; it comes into being under pressure and is forced by this pressure upward toward the surface of the earth. Lonegren and his colleagues in the American Society of Dowsers have been engaged for several decades in the use of dowsing techniques to detect and map various types of earth energy lines. These lines, according to Lonegren and others, are reflected or marked on the earth's surface by various alignments of sacred sites. See also Mitchell, *The View over Atlantis*, for a thorough discussion of these notions, especially the surface alignment of sites called ley lines.

2. Butler, *Ten Thousand Saints*, p. 174.

3. Delaney, *Dictionary of Saints*, p. 228.

4. Turner and Turner, *Image and Pilgrimage in Christian Culture*, p. 135.

5. Ibid.

6. Ibid., pp. 136, 135.

7. Ibid., p. 136.

8. Ó hAodha, *Bethu Brigte*, pp. 20–35, 605.

9. Curtayne, *St. Brigid of Ireland*, p. 84.

10. Rolleston, *Celtic Myths and Legends*, p. 425.

11. Montague, *Faber Book of Irish Verse*, p. 87.

12. Ó hAodha, *Bethu Brigte*, pp. 20–23.

13. MacNeill, *The Festival of Lughnasa*, pp. 275–86.

14. Ibid., pp. 277, 2, 5.

15. Rees and Rees, *Celtic Heritage*, p. 163.

16. Ibid., p. 160.

17. See O'Rahilly, *Early Irish History and Mythology*, pp. 472, 58.

18. Butler, *Ten Thousand Saints*, p. 112.

19. O'Rahilly, *Early Irish History and Mythology*, p. 469.

20. Ibid., p. 472.

6. Mary as the Lady at the Well in Modern Ireland

1. Ó hAodha, *Bethu Brigte*, pp. 25, 27, 29.

2. MacNeill, *The Festival of Lughnasa*, p. 607.

3. Pádraic Scanlon lives at 51 St. Bridget Place in Sligo. A coincidence of Bridget and Mary?

4. Ross, *Pagan Celtic Britain*, p. 226.

5. This information was gathered from Zimdars-Swartz, *Popular Devotion to the Virgin*, pp. 126–28.

6. See Powell, *The Celts*, pp. 147–48, for a discussion of votive deposits in pools, swamps, and bogs.

7. See Brenneman, *Spirals*, p. 65, for a discussion of the notion of natural and synthetic symbols as well as "whole meaning." See also Zimdars-Swartz, *Encountering Mary*, for an in-depth analysis of Marian apparitions including the reported event at Mount Melleray.

8. See Markale, *Celtic Civilization*, p. 24, for a discussion of the symbolic identity of spring with vagina, or *yoni*.

9. Deevy, *Our Blessed Lady Is Speaking to You*, pp. 19, 23.

10. Ibid., p. 72.

11. Ibid., pp. 26, 29.

12. Ibid., pp. 26, 30.

Bibliography

Arabagian, Ruth K. "Cattle Raiding and Bride Stealing." *Religion* 14 (1984): 107–42.

d'Arbois de Jubainville, Henry, trans. *The Irish Mythological Cycle.* Dublin: Hodges Figgis and Co., 1924.

Bleakley, Alan. *The Fruits of the Moon Tree.* London: Gateway Books, 1984.

Brenneman, Mary and Walter L., Jr. "Ireland: Land of Eternal Youth." In Luther H. Martin and James Goss, eds., *Essays on Jung and the Study of Religion.* Lanham, Md.: University Press of America, 1985.

Brenneman, Walter L., Jr. "Serpents, Cows, and Ladies: Contrasting Symbolism in Irish and Indo-European Cattle Raiding Myths." *History of Religions* 28 (1989): 340–54.

———, *Spirals: A Study in Symbol, Myth, and Ritual.* Lanham, Md.: University Press of America, 1977.

———, and Stanley Yarian. *The Seeing Eye: Hermeneutical Phenomenology in the Study of Religion.* University Park: Pennsylvania State University Press, 1982.

Butler, Hubert. *Ten Thousand Saints: A Study in Irish and European Origins.* Freshford: Wellbrook Press, 1972.

Chadwick, Nora. *The Celts.* New York: Penguin Books, 1970.

Curtayne, Alice. *St. Brigid of Ireland.* New York: Sheed and Ward, 1954.

Deevy, William, ed. *Our Blessed Lady Is Speaking to You. Are You Listening? Her Message from Melleray Grotto.* Privately printed, 1990.

Delaney, John J. *Dictionary of Saints.* New York: Doubleday, 1980.

Dillon, Myles. *The Cycles of the Kings.* London: Oxford University Press, 1946.

———, and Nora Chadwick. *Celtic Realms.* London: Weidenfeld and Nicholson, 1967.

Draak, M. *The Sacral Kingship.* Leiden: E. J. Brill, 1959.

Dumezil, Georges. *The Destiny of a King.* Chicago: University of Chicago Press, 1973.

Eliade, Mircea. *Cosmos and History.* New York: Harper and Row, 1954.

———. *Patterns in Comparative Religion.* Cleveland: Meridian, 1963.

Evans, Estyn. *Irish Folk Ways.* London: Routledge and Kegan Paul, 1957.

Foucault, Michel. *The Order of Things.* New York: Vintage Books, 1973.

Gwynn, Edward. *The Metrical Dindshenchas.* Dublin: Hodges Figgis and Co., 1924.

Hall, James, ed. *Dictionary of Subjects and Symbols in Art.* New York: Harper and Row, 1974.

Hood, A. B. E. *St. Patrick and His Writings.* London: Phillimore, 1978.

Husserl, Edmund. *The Idea of Phenomenology.* The Hague: Martinus Nijhoff, 1964.

Hutton, Ronald. *The Pagan Religions of the Ancient British Isles.* Oxford: Basil Blackwell, 1991.

Jensen, Adolph. *Myth and Cult among Primitive Peoples.* Chicago: University of Chicago Press, 1951.

Joyce, P. W. *Social History of Ancient Ireland.* London: Longmans Green and Company, 1903.

Kinsella, Thomas, trans. *The Tain.* London: Oxford University Press, 1969.

Livingstone, E. A. *The Concise Oxford Dictionary of the Christian Church.* London: Oxford University Press, 1977.

Logan, Patrick. *The Holy Wells of Ireland.* Gerrards Cross: Colin Smythe, 1980.

Lonegren, Sig. *Spiritual Dowsing.* Glastonbury: Gothic Image Publications, 1984.

Long, Charles. *Alpha: The Myths of Creation.* New York: George Braziller, 1963.

Lucas, A. T. "The Sacred Trees of Ireland." *Cork Historical and Archaeological Society* 68 (1963): 16–54.

Macalister, R. A. S. *Tara, a Pagan Sanctuary of Ancient Ireland.* New York: Charles Scribner's Sons, 1931.

Mac Cana, P. *Celtic Mythology.* London: Hamlyn Publishing Group, 1970.

MacNeill, Máire. *The Festival of Lughnasa.* London: Oxford University Press, 1962.

Markale, Jean. *Celtic Civilization.* London: Gordon J. Cremonesi, 1978.

Mitchell, John. *The View over Atlantis.* London: Thames and Hudson, 1969.

Montague, John, ed. *Faber Book of Irish Verse.* London: Faber and Faber, 1978.

Neumann, Erich. *The Great Mother.* Princeton, N.J.: Princeton University Press, 1974.

O'Donovan, John, ed. *The Annals of the Kingdom of Ireland by the Four Masters from the Earliest Period to the Year 1616.* Dublin: Hodges Smith Co., 1856.

——, ed. *Tracts Relating to Ireland.* Dublin: Irish Archaeological Society, 1841.

Ó hAodha, Donncha, ed. *Bethu Brigte.* Dublin: Dublin Institute for Advanced Studies, 1978.

Ó hÓgáin, Dáithí. *Myth, Legend, and Romance: An Encyclopaedia of the Irish Folk Tradition.* London: Ryan Publishing Co., 1990.

O'Rahilly, Thomas F. *Early Irish History and Mythology.* Dublin: Dublin Institute for Advanced Studies, 1964.

Powell, T. G. E. *The Celts.* London: Thames and Hudson, 1958.

Rees, Alwyn, and Brinley Rees. *Celtic Heritage.* New York: Thames and Hudson, 1961.

Rolleston, T. W. *Celtic Myths and Legends.* London: Bracken Books, 1985.

Ross, Anne. *Pagan Celtic Britain.* London: Routledge and Kegan Paul, 1969.

Seaman, D., and R. Mugerauer, eds. *Dwelling Place and Environment: Towards a Phenomenology of Person and World.* The Hague: Martinus Nijhoff, 1985.

Sjoestedt, Maire-Louise. *Gods and Heroes of the Celts.* Berkeley, Calif.: Turtle Island Foundation, 1982.

Stokes, Whitley, trans. *The Tripartite Life of Patrick.* London: Cyebra and Spottiswoode, 1887.

Turner, Victor, and Edith Turner. *Image and Pilgrim-*

age in Christian Culture. New York: Columbia University Press, 1978.

Zimdars-Swartz, Sandra L. *Encountering Mary: From La Salette to Medjugorje.* Princeton, N.J.: Princeton University Press, 1991.

———. *Popular Devotion to the Virgin: The Marian Phenomena at Melleray, Republic of Ireland.* Extrait des Archives de Sciences Sociales des Religions, no. 67/1. Montrouge, France. 1989.

Index

DATE DUE			
			Printed in USA